JUST

DRIVING

TO

THRIVING

Praise for *Just Driving to Thriving*

Jeff's ideas are spot on....easy to implement with profound effect. The idea of getting 10% freer is all it takes to make a huge difference, allowing for better decision making, a calmer approach and an opportunity to become more thoughtful. *Just Driving to Thriving* is a key tool for anyone looking to get perspective and to give themselves a break. – **Rabbi Richard Tobias**, Congregations Beth Torah

Jeff's book teaches you how to build a vessel for compound growth. He has done a superb job combining both old wisdom and modern tools to achieve living a life of higher consciousness. – **Gedale Fenster**, Motivational Speaker

Knowing Jeff for almost five decades, I have seen first hand his transformation and can say with confidence that *Just Driving to Thriving* is a game changer! – **Joseph L. Jerome**, President/Co-Founder at Jemb Realty Corp.

Just Driving to Thriving is the !!! (exclamation point) on what Jeff has made his life's mission in being a man of service. The teachings and knowledge in this book are priceless, and I urge you and your teams to learn them! – **Harry Adjmi** CEO One Step Up LTD

With *Just Driving to Thriving*, Jeff Sitt has created a way forward for us all. For anyone who wants to live with more peace, purpose, and passion for life, this is your book. Jeff turns the process of freeing oneself from the emotional and spiritual blockages that limit us, into a road trip we can't wait to embark on! – **Alice Chera**, Life Coach & Consultant

Jeff Sitt guides us on a road trip where every stop is another opportunity for growth and self discovery and he presents these truths in digestible easy to follow prompts. – **Vivien Hidary**, Teacher & Inspiration Speaker

JUST
DRIVING
TO
THRIVING

A LEADERSHIP GUIDE TO DECREASE
STRESS AND INCREASE PROFITS

JEFF SITT

BIG MOOSE
PUBLISHING

Published by: Big Moose Publishing
PO Box 127 Site 601 RR#6 Saskatoon, SK CANADA S7K3J9
www.bigmoosepublishing.com

Printed in Canada.

ISBN: 978-1-989840-33-7 (hardcover)
ISBN: 978-1-989840-31-3 (softcover)
ISBN: 978-1-989840-32-0 (ebook)

Big Moose Publishing 11/2021

DEDICATION

To my beautiful wife and best friend, Rochelle, who opened the door for me to come out of the shadows and be myself.

CONTENTS

INTRODUCTION

Buckle up! You're about to take an amazing journey, driving away from worry and fear toward a life of purpose and peace.

Of course, as a leader you already know all about crazy rides: nerve-wracking decisions, skipped weekends, nighttime worries—the list goes on. But this ride is different. This time you're on your way to learning how to fully engage with life in a way that keeps you from repeating mistakes and making new ones. You're on your way to embracing your potential and thriving.

We're all leaders at heart. Whether you're a business owner, CEO, middle manager or a leader in your own life and community, day-to-day living can be a stressful business. Along the way, you've picked up some bad habits—lingering mistakes/worries/resentments/fears that keep you from connecting with others and enjoying the abundance you deserve.

What's the solution? Just get 10% freer.

Why 10% Freer?
Wait a minute, you say. Why just 10% freer? I mean, why not

50% freer or 100% freer? Sounds good, right?

Over the years, I've learned from working with scores of clients (and myself) that anything more is difficult to achieve. 10% is attainable.

Does that mean I'm advocating mediocrity? Not on your life! And it doesn't mean you stop at 10%. Once you have the magic of momentum working with you, you can go on and on to achieve more and more freedom. But if you don't start small— you won't ever start. I know you know what I'm talking about.

Free from what?

What do you need to get free of? Well, for starters, that noisy backseat driver living in your head, yelling at you at every turn and stoplight. You know, that voice inside you that says you're not good enough, not man enough, not happy enough, not sexy enough, not tall enough, not smart enough, not free enough, not good looking enough, not, not, not ... I could write hundreds of *not enoughs*.

Folks, it's time to expose that troublemaker!

Too bad you can't kill him, replace him, divorce him. Nope. It's a life sentence. So let's take him out of the confines of the backseat so he can be seen and roam about. He's been cooped up for so long he's gotten very angry and keeps sliding notes across the front seat to get your attention. When that didn't work he started kicking the back of your seat, and then outright banging and screaming.

As if that's not bad enough, that annoying backseat driver makes you do all kinds of crazy stuff: yell at others, take drugs, break up, move to other states, quit jobs, steal. Even kill! Some people decide to jump off a bridge because the backseat driver said this world would be better off without them. Ever hear someone say, "The voice made me do it."? Yep, that's what I'm talking about.

Of course, this problem isn't new. It's been around for as long as our brains have been firing synapses. Backseat drivers have done tremendous damage in this world: wars, rape, crime, depression, drug addiction, you name it. That bully has wreaked havoc all over the place from the beginning of time. Co-existing with this out-of-control maniac is like living life under a dictatorship of negativity and unworthiness.

What's it like living 10% freer?

Words, books and movies can't explain or demonstrate what life can be like when you're living just 10% freer. Each moment will be the greatest of your life. And that, my friends, is a life worth working for.

For starters, you'll be free from excessive worry, anxiety and fear. What comes in its place is clarity, calm and courage. The day flows in magnificent ways. You will navigate complicated business decisions with ease and comfort. As a leader, you will find you are much more efficient and productive. As a result, you'll start noticing an increase in creative solutions, which in turn, leads to an increase in profits.

Have you ever been in a negotiation with a vendor or client where the uncertainty and anxiety were off the charts? Then you leave that meeting and in your next conversation you erupt or boil inside and just shut down? That is a direct result of not being 10% freer. And the ripple effect doesn't stop there. Think about what those interactions do to the morale and productivity of your team, and possibly later to your family when you get home.

On a more everyday level, ask yourself how many times you've walked into a coffee shop and gotten irritated that the person in front of you is paying with change? You give an OMG look to the person behind you as you start to churn inside because you *need* to get to work! Who was in control of you? Yep, your backseat driver. And here's the kicker—you likely didn't even know he was there. You think and believe all this is coming from you!

Look at a child of 2 to 3 years old. They flow so beautifully. It is a joy to watch. Why? They have no blockages. When they are sad they cry, when happy they laugh, when they are silly they are silly. They don't stop and think things like: *Am I making a fool of myself? Will my boss fire me? Will my boyfriend think I'm immature?* Young children are blockless; they flow with life. Us adults? We need to work on all the plaque and gunk we've built over the years so that we can flow once again.

When you get free from that—even just 10% free—life becomes a joy again. And as you work on becoming 10% freer, you can go on to become 12, 15, 20% freer. Along the way, you come to the realization that life is a lot better unblocked. You may see a sunset that will be the most beautiful sunset you've ever seen. You may be stuck in negotiating a contract with a supplier and get this feeling of joy and ecstasy for no apparent reason. You may have an issue that needs some discovery and contemplation to solve, but first you decide to release your anxiety about the issue and, bam! The solution just pops into your lap.

Wonder why? Because you gave life room to present itself to you. Then you'll find your spiritual arteries get larger and healthier and the flow of life just moves through you. You decide then and there to floss your spiritual arteries on a daily basis so that the plaque releases and makes room for love, joy, and enthusiasm that grows and grows.

What inspired this book?

When I wrote this book, I felt a strong sense that I needed to follow my higher power. In my Jewish faith, that is God or Hashem, which in Hebrew literally means "the name," referring to God. This is the guiding light in my life. But as you read, you can substitute whatever works for you: higher power, universe, energy, light, source. While these concepts are as big as the universe, their differences are small. Don't let terminology stop you from enjoying the benefits of living *10% freer.*

In many faiths, the concept of 10% shows up often. In Jewish law, for example, it is strongly suggested to give ma'aser or 10% of annual earnings to charity for the less fortunate. That number—10%—is attainable to all. Whether you're a farmer in Israel, a banker in New York, or you just won the lottery, the mitzvah (doing a good deed) of separating ma'aser will apply to you in a particular way.

The 10% we give is actually an investment in ourselves. That investment pays tremendous dividends—what I call the 10/10/10 rule. That is, as we give away 10% of our uncomfortableness, we become 10% freer, which leads us to being 10% closer to Hashem! Who wouldn't want that?

The light is always on.

The light of the Creator is always on, just like the sun is always shining above the clouds, even on the cloudiest of days. But connecting to that light is not always simple. Some believe that thinking positive thoughts will connect them to it. Or meditating will, omming the world away.

Or taking drugs, psychedelics mushrooms and other mind-altering substances. Those things might give some freedom, but unfortunately, these are all temporary remedies. (Believe me, I've tried them all.)

I call these approaches "spiritual bypasses." What I mean is we acknowledge that we have a problem and a need to connect with the light to help fix the problem. But they bypass the necessary steps of learning, understanding and experiencing in order to integrate the essence of being free.

Many times when clients come for a consultation, they often ask, "OK, so what's the answer?" They want that one-step solution to all their problems—NOW. Lose 30 pounds in 30 minutes! Six-pack abs in six minutes.

Earlier I said the light of the Creator is always on—but that doesn't mean all we need to do is plug in and voilà, poof, nirvana! The real answer comes when we understand and learn for ourselves what is blocking that light from our lives. Without self-discovery, we don't have a clue what is standing in the way of the light. When ignored, these blockages build up and eventually burst into anger, resentment, depressions, health issues, drug use, or worse, suicide.

Even the most accomplished of us can reach a point where one or more aspects of our life isn't going according to plan. Something is slowing us down, getting in our way or stopping us. Our handbrake is on, but we don't know why.

That's where this book comes in.

Just Driving to Thriving combines evidence-based science and spiritual teachings with powerful coaching to free your body, mind and spirit so you can accelerate your journey to a more successful and meaningful life.

If you're stuck, if the road isn't clear, or if you're at a crossroads with too many choices, then you've come to the right place. You will be able to create a customized program to help you rediscover your power and set you on the road to healthy relationships, strong self-worth and lasting serenity.

Why me?

So you may be asking why you should listen to what I have to say. Good question. Fact is I do not have any PhDs, I did not win the Nobel peace prize and Oprah has not called me yet.

But I did run a wholesale company that was responsible for producing over one billion dollars in retail sales and a successful real estate business, to name just a couple of organizations I've been a leader in.

I know how busy you can get; so busy you take too many wrong turns and find yourself at a dead end. That was me about 10 years ago when I was in a terrible "accident" (to keep our car metaphor going). My transmission—spiritual, intellectual, emotional—was shot, and my finances were in the tank. As if things couldn't get worse, I was at the end of a 27-year marriage. It was not hyperbole to say I was totaled, wrecked, mangled.

For a while, I refused to address what was going on, living life primarily from the outside and thinking that that would solve everything. It didn't. It doesn't.

Then one day, this wreck of a car just stopped. I couldn't move forward. I was in the darkest place of my entire life. I recall being at a magnificent wedding reception at one of the nicest hotels in Manhattan. The next day, a few people still around after the wedding went to a breakfast to celebrate the bride and groom. And in this beautiful white room in the Pierre Hotel, with gorgeous, bright October light pouring in, I was at the unhappiest moment of my entire life. While everyone around me rejoiced, I felt desperate and completely, internally bankrupt. All I could see inside my mind was what was going to be written on my tombstone: Jeff died broke, unhappy and lived a life without purpose.

I was 53 years old, and I thought my life was over.

Somehow, though, I began to crowbar my way out. I knew I needed help.

And I got it. Through that journey over 10 years with lots of exploration, learning, and reading, I have been born again. Yep, I've been born again. And during that time, my grandkids were born, awakening me to the joys of living in the moment, living a life beyond my wildest imagination.

I am now remarried for seven years to the love of my life. I honestly pinch myself each morning watching my wife sleep. And I have a wonderful relationship with my ex-wife, four magnificent sons, two amazing daughter-in-laws and, at the moment of writing this book, two grandkids. Life is magnificent.

I've been through a lot of stalls, wrecks, wrong turns and detours. And I'll keep clearing out blockages and cleaning my windshield. The way I see it, it ain't over 'til I'm dead and buried. So until that time, I'm going to keep doing what I'm doing, loving my family, loving life.

> "True love is a love of giving, not a love of receiving."
> ~ Rabbi Abraham Twerski[AH']

Ready for this road trip?

As you read through this book, you'll notice I make a lot of analogies to cars. I found this to be an amazingly apt metaphor for our lives, our bodies, and our minds.

Think about it. You need your engine to purr to maintain your health. You want a clear windshield to see the world as it truly is. And to successfully travel through life, you need to get rid of all that gunk lining your pipes, keep your windshield clean and release the handbrake so that you can get where you want to go.

> "You have brains in your head. You have feet in your shoes. You can steer yourself any direction you choose." ~ Dr. Seuss

The road map

The key concepts in this book are about you. As I just mentioned, I often refer to you as the car and everything going inside of it. If you take this ride with me, you'll learn who is really driving your car. (If you're like me, you're going to be surprised!) You'll identify that backseat driver and other pre-installed programming—and discover how to make it all work for you.

Along the way, you'll learn about the road of life, and why you seem to be driving over so many potholes and repeatedly getting into accidents. I'll share some new driving techniques as well as how to use your growing awareness to clean and demist your windows. It's virtually impossible to drive when you have all that bug gunk on your windshield that's been accumulating for years. Or when you keep turning your head to listen to that nutcase in the backseat who's always telling you what is wrong with you, what is going to be wrong, and even worse, how bad you drove yesterday!

The good news is that it's not going to take that long to clean up your car and get it running smoother. You don't need a new model—just a few visits to the repair shop to fix, clean, and shine your car—dents and all.

So let's get started. Here's what's on the road ahead:

1.   WHAT'S UNDER THE HOOD?: You'll find out just how powerful you really are. Your mind and body are the vehicle in which you live your life, and you'll learn some of the science and chemistry about how it all works. You'll see what drives your thinking and emotions, and you'll be able to take back control and become a master of your biology.

2.   PRIMING YOUR VEHICLE: The first step in learning how to let go of what is holding you back is to understand who is doing the holding. The constant traffic

of thoughts is so distracting that it is difficult to know who you really are. It turns out the question "Who am I?" is a deep one that takes time and clarity to answer. You'll begin to explore who you are and what your relationship is to your thoughts, emotions and the outside world.

3. DEMISTING YOUR WINDSHIELD: Over the years, your windshield has become encrusted with splats and dirt. You'll learn ways to clean it off that bring a clarity to your life like you've never experienced before.

4. CONTROLLING YOUR BACKSEAT DRIVER: We can willfully generate thoughts, but most of the time we hear incessant personal chatter from that noisy bully— the backseat driver. Where do all those thoughts come from, and are they actually increasing or diminishing your chance for happiness?

5. FINDING A NEW DIRECTION: Set a course to develop new thoughts, behaviors and actions. You'll get started on the journey to a new you. Get ready to rock!

6. SIMONIZING THE OPERATING SYSTEM IN YOUR CAR: The human mind is truly amazing— brilliant and creative, and yet it can be the source of great personal suffering and pain. Get free of this pain and start programming your GPS to work for you. You'll explore what the mind is and why it creates the thoughts it does.

7. TAKING CARE OF YOUR ENGINE: The engine that keeps us ticking also creates the emotions that sometimes overwhelm us. Becoming comfortable with the full range of emotions and energies the heart creates is the prerequisite to true liberation. You'll learn how to clear the gunk out of your spiritual pipes and keep your engine purring.

8.   FIXING PAST ROAD TRIPS: Uncover the stored messages from your past that are running your life. Learn how these patterns are created and the difficulties they can cause. What would happen if you decided to free yourself of these past patterns instead of using life to compensate for them?

9.   TAKING THE HANDBRAKE OFF: True spiritual growth is not about getting anything—it is always about release. Free yourself from the habitual thoughts and behaviors that have stopped you in the past. Letting go is the highest spiritual path there is.

10. DEALING WITH OTHER TRAFFIC ON THE ROAD: Along the way, you'll grow more comfortable with situations you encounter on your journey. Acceptance is a major step in letting go and surrendering. We'll explore your place in the outside world and what your relationship to it should be.

11. PUTTING YOUR PEDAL TO THE METAL: The ultimate step—going for it! Hit the road to find your purpose and grow into your potential. You'll begin to put in place strategies for dealing with relationships, career and yourself.

12. ROLLING DOWN THE FREEWAY OF LIFE: Once you start getting serious about your inner work, you'll begin to understand the power you have to cruise in a state of freedom—both inside and out. You will learn to live in harmony with the flow of life—free of anxiety and full of tremendous joy within.

And one more thing: *Just Driving to Thriving* is a small book by design. A long book about small changes didn't make sense to me. Instead, I wanted to offer these ideas in an easy-to-read format so that you can get started right away making small changes (for big results).

1% FREER:
WHAT'S BLOCKING
YOUR PATH?

What's keeping you from living a fuller, freer, fulfilling life?

One of the biggest obstacles you face is this crazy idea we all have that the world needs to spin at the perfect speed and our boss/kids/car/clothes/dinner/umbrella/news/government/traffic/subway/weather need to be exactly the way we expect—OR ELSE!

Do you see the pattern? If you're like most of us, you walk around your life looking at what's *not* happening the way you want. When it doesn't, you get dizzy/angry/frustrated. You fall down yelling at life—and blaming it for your fall!

What's going on? Well, it's the *Yetzer Hara*, (evil inclination aka Satan or dark energy) in Jewish tradition, the opposite is *Yetzer Hatov* (good inclination). Other names for this include dark energy and EGO or "Edging God Out." Whatever you call it, it's stolen your attention and can lead you into painful situations.

But when you step back and take a clear-headed look at the whole scenario, you realize it can be boiled down to one and only one problem: You.

Why you? Because you're looking in the wrong direction— outside yourself. Well, newsflash—the outside will never, ever sustain long-term freedom because you have no control over the outside world. You don't have a say in how your customer's life is going or how fast the barista is working or who decided to get a flat tire when you needed traffic to flow nicely.

That's why the only direction you should be facing is *inside*. Yep, inside *you*. You have all the power, joy and wisdom within to break free from the insanity.

Let's dig a little deeper into this idea with an analogy. When you go home at night do you leave your car windows and doors open with your car keys on the dashboard? When you go to sleep do you leave your home's windows and doors open with all your most precious valuables on the kitchen table with a sign saying "take me"? I can almost hear you shouting, "Jeff, are you some kind of a nut?"

OK, but if you're like a lot of folks, that is exactly what you're doing with the most valuable possession you've got: your soul. In our culture, thieves are always prowling about, trying to steal. It's like one of the oldest cons known to man, a street game called Three Card Monty. You can find it set up on a cardboard box on city sidewalks all over the world. As the name implies, it's played with just three cards (two are the same, one is different), and the goal is for the Dealer to get you, the Mark, hooked on making a fast and easy buck. Heck, all you have to do is pick the one different card out of three. And all the Dealer does is simply play leapfrog with the cards right in front of you. Sounds simple, right? It's not! I was taken for 300 bucks in a matter of two minutes when I was 21 years old on the streets of New York, right in front of the Empire State Building. Wake up folks! This is the same principle Madison Avenue, politicians, con artists, you name it, build their game on.

On the television they use four very powerful words—"Stay Tuned for More"—to keep you watching so the next Dealer in line, a.k.a. Madison Avenue commercials, can scare the bejesus out of you or make your mouth water with food ladened with salt and sugar. You, the Mark, are just too busy looking in the wrong direction, thanks to the willingness of the Dealer, to notice you're being ripped off! I know you've heard this many, many times before, but now you know the real name of the game.

It's time to start taking control of your life. And you can do it. Along the way, you'll learn acceptance of the world just the way it is. No, this doesn't mean you sit back and let the world happen *to* you. It means you take responsibility for this dance you're in with life. Up to this point, you've allowed life to take the lead. Now it's time to take it back and pay attention to what's going on—inside and outside of your life. And with this understanding comes a tremendous ability to get out of the jail in your mind that you call the world.

"Your time is limited, so don't waste it living someone else's life. Don't be trapped by...living with the results of other people's thinking."
~Steve Jobs

TOTALLY BACKWARDS CONCEPT #1: You're in the driver's seat.

I hate to break it you, folks, but more than likely if you're reading this book, you're not in the driver's seat of your life. Oh sure, parents, teachers, bosses love to tell you that you are—and that all your screwups are because you're *not* driving in the right direction (i.e. *their* direction).

Truth is, no one can steer in the right direction from the backseat, which is where you're trapped when you're listening more to these outsiders than inside your own heart and mind. As a result, the outside world can twist and turn your life in directions you never wanted.

Of course, life will always surprise us. Like John Lennon's famous saying that "Life is what happens when you're busy making other plans." Your parents died; you didn't get into the school you wanted; you lost that business deal; you can't seem to make friends. These are all detours presented for you to work with, not to play the poor-me game. That game is unwinnable. People spend their entire lives looking, talking and fantasizing about *what if* they were born rich, *what if* they'd married better, *what if* they'd taken that other job, *what if* I didn't sell Apple @$38?

Instead, I want you to hop into the front seat, plant your hands firmly on the steering wheel and go!

How? By becoming aware of what's going on *inside* you.

It's Not the Cards You Were Dealt—But How You Play Your Hand.

We're all dealt a hand of cards when we're born. Your world started with the parents you were born to, the shape of your body, the color of your hair, the school you went to, the neighborhood you played in, and guess what? You had no control over those. Later in life, disappointments mount—you didn't get the job you wanted, your girlfriend left you, you're living in a home different from what you'd hoped for.

If we're not careful, we can play out our lives limited by that hand. But what a waste of your precious life! I'm not disrespecting what has happened to you. I just want to help you see a different path. Because once you realize you *do* have control over how you deal with the hand you were dealt, well, now that's freedom!

The question isn't the hand you were dealt but how you play the hand. Your job is to work with what you've got and understand what's going on. You see, life can and should be a fun game. And it can be when you're ready, willing and able to consciously use the cards that work for you and discard the ones that don't. After all, they're only cards.

And be on the lookout for what cards are coming next. Get

excited about what life will show you today. Maybe you'll get lucky and be presented with a smelly, yucky card. Oh boy, what a gift! (Painful, yes, but a gift just that same.)

When you see life from this perspective, you will naturally raise yourself to a higher, lighter level. I don't mean enlightenment—that's a state of consciousness for beings much higher than I ever hope to achieve! No, I'm talking about light-fullness, i.e., being in a lighter, liberated state. Life flows, you see rich colors, you taste exquisite flavors, you feel the wind, gentle and strong. This is the gift of being alive.

NEXT STEP

Pay attention to your cards and resist the urge to play the Why Me Game. Instead, transition to the Welcome Game. Start today with one card, e.g., fear, jealousy, self-doubt, etc., and pay close attention to it. Accept it as a part of you, but don't accept that you can't do anything with it. What is the hurt? Get clear and name it. Is it fear, loneliness, embarrassment? How has it helped you? Is it still a useful card, or is it time to discard it? You will learn in the coming chapters that on a deep level your feelings are all very useful. Again, the question isn't the cards you were dealt but how you play them!

Get excited about what life will show you today.

TOTALLY BACKWARDS CONCEPT #2: You're doing just fine the way you are.

Maybe some folks are doing things right, but it's been my experience, through my clients and certainly my own life, that we were never taught how to live freely.

Your pipes are blocked.

Like a car with sludge in its engine, soul stones have formed in your spiritual arteries and are clogging them. Things got clogged because no one taught you what to do with the information and misinformation that is constantly hurtling toward you. I hate to tell you, but as a result of this onslaught, you've got some hardened plaque inside you.

To better understand how this plays out in life, consider this scenario:

The driver in front of you is double-parked and blocking your way; your internal temperature rises and you become angry, frustrated and resentful. Sound familiar? Time passes, no movement. You honk your horn, your face turns red and you yell and curse about what a jerk that person is.

What's at play here, deep at your core?

It's not the driver that's the issue. The blockage is created by what this scenario brings up in *you*—from *inside* you. Since it's next to impossible to find the root of your issue in that moment, let's fast forward and watch a video replay of the event. As you watch, ask yourself what you were honestly feeling at the moment your temperature started to rise. Maybe you had an important appointment or needed to pick up a friend to head to the airport, and this doubled-parked car was messing with that. But often, if you look honestly, you might discover that you were feeling anxious and/or fearful *before* the anger and resentment settled in. Bingo! Drill down on that to start to clear a blockage in your spiritual arteries.

So let's replay that scene, but this time you're coming from a new state of light-fullness. As you approach the doubled-park car, you notice you're becoming agitated. You have someplace to be and this is literally blocking your path. But today you're more experienced and conscious. You automatically take a breath or two and start to recognize what's happening inside you and today it happens to be anxiousness. So you take a step back. You go inside yourself and relax your neck and shoulders, close your eyes and release that feeling to God, the universe, or just the air around you. You do this a few more times, if needed, and open your eyes. Now you're ready to come at this scene from a relaxed, centered and much less anxious space. You call your friend to say that you might be a few minutes late. And while you wait, you notice the exquisite iridescence of a blue jay in a tree next to the double-parked car.

Over time, you'll gain an understanding about these blockages, and with that understanding, you'll start to take responsibility and stop the blame game. You'll better understand how to drive your car, which you've driven since you were a teenager, only now you'll take responsibility for your driving and how you're going to get where *you* want to go. I'm sorry to say that some folks are stuck in the blame game with the poor-me traffic jam in their minds their whole life! That does not need to be you.

NEXT STEP

Pay attention to what makes you angry today. When your anger flares, step back a moment, take a deep breath, and ask yourself what's really at play. This isn't to deny that your experience is frustrating (card you're dealt), but you do have a choice about how to react (how you play that card). Take a few more deep, centering breaths. From that more relaxed place, ask yourself what next steps would get you closer to what you want.

CASE STUDY

Joseph was struggling to keep up. His boss, owner of a fast-growing company with staffing mushrooming from 30 to 80, sent Joseph to me because he was not upgrading his work level or his professionalism. Don't get me wrong—Joseph was a very creative, capable person, but he was having a hard time integrating into the company as it became increasingly corporate. And he was missing deadlines due to his lack of organization and other necessary skills.

Joseph and I got together so that I could begin to understand what was blocking his path. He told me about his job and that he was 38, married, with two kids. So far so good. As we talked, though, I could clearly see that he was experiencing deep problems.

"You're out of control," I told him. He looked at me perplexed and perturbed. I went on. "Let me ask you a question: Do you ever wake up in fear, anger, frustration, confusion, anxiety?"

He nervously wrung his hands as he looked at me and answered, "Every single day."

"Then you are totally out of control because you're not driving your car—you know, the vehicle of *you*. You are not in the driver's seat. What is in the driver's seat is fear, anger, frustration, confusion and anxiety. So, you're just in the backseat being driven every day to Fear Town. And every turn you take in this town is Anger Alley, Frustration Freeway, Confusion Corner, Anxiety Avenue and so on."

Joseph didn't have a problem with what I said. No, he agreed. Trouble was, he blamed everything and everyone else for his woes. He wasn't getting the right cooperation from this place or that. And his wife? Oh, she wasn't doing this, but she was doing that. And he wasn't getting good direction from the executives. It became clear to me that Joseph was not only not in the driver's seat, he was blaming everybody around him for the reason why his car was stuck in a ditch.

We worked together, and to his credit, Joseph kept coming in. I gave him some of the exercises in this book and all the help I could throw at him. The first 10 minutes of his sessions were filled with complaining and complaining and more complaining. That went on for four months until I finally told his superiors they were wasting their money. Joseph was in complete and utter denial; he was out of control, which reflected something serious going on inside him.

This is a painful way to live life. Sure, we all have times in our lives when we take the victim role. But that way of life simply doesn't work if you want to live a life filled with creativity, joy and happiness.

If you picked up this book, I believe there is a part of you, at some level, that wants to start taking responsibility for your journey in this life. Unfortunately, that wasn't the case for Joseph. Eventually he was fired. As he walked out of the building, he was still blaming everything and everyone. To me this is tragic—for Joseph and the company, because he was very creative, but could not live up to his potential.

So, his blockage—like gunky oil in a car's engine (which you will read about later)—was so thick that he was stuck. He couldn't take ownership or responsibility, for whatever reason, to move on to the next chapter of his life, which could have been beautiful for him. But that was his choice.

Don't make it yours.

Like a car with sludge in the engine, soul stones have formed in your spiritual arteries.

TOTALLY BACKWARDS CONCEPT #3: You're a victim of your past.

The biology of you often means your life experiences keep repeating themselves—differently but from the same root. They keep on releasing hormones that keep you in jail.

We are chemically conditioned.

Biology plays a huge role in how you react and navigate your world. We are born with an internal survival mechanism for the sole purpose of physical preservation. This auto survival mechanism is on autopilot and at work all day, every day. You don't see what goes on behind the scenes inside your body. (Maybe that's just as well because if you did, your mind might explode!)

Consider this experience: You're walking into traffic while looking at your phone, and a driver in the car that is about to hit you blows her horn. Your internal system snaps into overdrive and within a nanosecond your body jumps back to avoid being hit. Then, that woman has the nerve to give you the "what are you, a moron?" look. That sets off chemicals inside your body. So many actions and transactions take place within three seconds that it would take a team of neuroscientists three chapters to explain everything that had just happened inside your brain and body. To put it bluntly, your butt just got saved, because whatever higher power works for you installed this amazing system inside you.

That's the good news.

The bad news? Every time you have a fearful thought about something in the future—that hasn't even happened yet— your body releases those same hormones because your body thinks it's about to be hit by a car. It's like having one foot on the gas of your car and the other on the brake. You want to move forward, but you're afraid or conditioned to fail, so you slam on the brakes. Needless to say, this is a very stressful, unhappy place to be.

How does this happen? No horn is being honked as you sit comfortably on your couch watching TV, but as soon as that commercial comes on talking about how bad the economy is and maybe you might need to file for bankruptcy, your heart starts to race, your breathing becomes shallow, and you get this feeling that your life as you know it is over. You don't realize it, but your body is receiving signals—just like those you got when you were about to be hit by a car—and within three seconds those same hormones that saved you from an actual accident get released. Only this time they don't save you—they hold you back.

Your brain is not the culprit. It's your conditioning from childhood (or even a past life, but let's not delve into that). Here's an example to explain what I mean.

You're 4 years old and your dad gets fired. You have no idea what's going on, but the look on his face is very scary. Over dinner, he yells at your mom for buying the better butter. Even if you don't remember it, this event leaves an impression on your subconscious. As years pass this scene plays out again and again on different stages with different actors, reinforcing this impression. Fast forward to when you're 35 years old. You're experiencing some financial issues in your life when that commercial comes on about bankruptcy, and without your even knowing it, you're back in your family home, just 4 years old and scared to death. And now you're thinking about making that call to the bankruptcy company that's trying to sell you freedom.

Don't get sucked in!

It's astonishing how often this pattern plays out. Without knowing it, that fear of losing a job or going into serious debt is running—and ruining—your life.

NEXT STEP

When you feel your body freeze, your heart hammer, your breath quicken, pay attention. This isn't always a negative occurrence. Maybe you see an artist working or a musician making her fiddle sing (the same instrument you played once upon a time). That can be a green light for delving deeper into your aspirations. But for now, I'm talking about the physical reactions to situations that are holding you back. When you can relax, replay what was going on when you felt afraid, nervous, or horrified. Sit quietly for as long as it takes to let a memory (or memories) bubble up. What do they reveal to you— and how can you say no to them? (We'll cover more of this later in the book.). Rich resources within are waiting for you to discover them.

1% FREER TAKEAWAYS:

1. Stop blaming the world. While we don't have control over the world as a whole, we do have control over how we react to life's twists and turns. Accept the hand you were dealt and take control of how you play it. Understand that it is the *Yetzer Hara* that wants to bring you down. That's the game of life.

2. Open up to what's going on inside you. Every day is a fresh opportunity to learn where you are headed and why you want to go there. Start to experience your life from the inside out. Bring that new perspective to everything that happens to you.

3. Accept that you've been chemically conditioned. Pay attention to how your body reacts to situations. Awaken to those stimuli so you can consciously move forward with your life's purpose.

2% FREER:
WHY DO WE SUFFER?

T he train is late. Your shirt shrank. He didn't put the toilet seat down... again! That car is driving too slow. Too fast. It's too hot, too cold, too rainy, too windy.

Sound familiar? All day long we're presented with opportunities to suffer. And boy, do we ever.

Gautama Buddha wrote the book, so to speak, on suffering. His First Noble Truth is typically translated as "All life involves suffering."

But I like to revise that truth a little and say that "Life presents suffering" is a more accurate translation. I think we can all agree that life offers plenty of opportunities for pain, stress and unhappiness!

So how do we live with this truth? First, by accepting it. Then, we can get better at dealing with the roadblocks and detours that come our way. Work every day to allow life, i.e., accept life's messiness. In my life, Judaism means living the faith. Religious Jews try to bring holiness into everything they do, by doing it as an act that praises God and honors everything God has done. For us, the whole of our lives becomes an act of worship.

That means you're not doing anything wrong (even though your parents/spouse/boss in the backseat keep telling you differently), you can't control what others do (things get all tangled up like a traffic jam when you try), and you can't make all of life's frustrations and disappointments go away (what a waste of precious time!). When you realize that, you begin to relax and let go.

Ahhh. That feels better already.

But acceptance doesn't mean we just roll over and succumb to suffering. We can practice ways to lessen the pain—and I don't mean by hiding in seclusion or taking drugs. When we learn more about what causes us pain and stress, we can deal with it head on. Once we do, the road ahead is a lot less bumpy.

Acceptance of life's messiness is a good start.

SELF-DISCOVERY STEP #1: Our biology works with us—and against us.

We came into this world with preset programming. The purpose of these biological programs is survival. Way back, when humans first began to progress, before we even had the capacity for language to communicate with other humans, this messaging system gave us ways to stay safe and self-regulate.

Like that scenario in the last chapter—a horn honks and you jump back to the curb in a nanosecond—that's your pre-installed system in action, no upgrades needed. There are hundreds of thousands of these auto-program systems taking place inside you, all day, every day. Thanks to these magnificent mechanisms, we've gone from outrunning saber-toothed tigers to building cities; designing cars, planes and trains; and launching people to the moon.

Even today with all our science and know-how, this walking, talking ingenious piece of machinery we call our bodies is so complex that mankind cannot build one. Doctors and scientists can perform open-heart surgery and invent lifesaving drugs, but this magnificent piece of engineering— our body—remains somewhat mysterious. In a word, it's a marvel.

So far so good …

It's a mind field out there.

So, yes, your body's preprogramming can be a godsend. But it can also direct you down the wrong path if you're not paying attention. That's when you lose your way. You try to stay safe by stepping lightly through life, hoping to avoid all those minefields that could blow up your world.

But who wants to tiptoe through life?

Instead, become conscious of what's going on inside so that you can walk with confidence. Travel back to your early years to find what I call your *mind* fields—that long list of experiences you don't want to repeat. Without your knowing it, they have become a deafening and deadening mantra repeated over and over throughout your life. *Better not speak up at work. I'm not good at social situations. I'll never talk with Uncle Joe again.*

Uh-oh, you're tiptoeing again. Which really only works for a while. You're going along, not making waves, until you hear that Uncle Joe's wife is planning his 70th birthday party. "NO WAY! I'm NOT going there!" you say to yourself, your heart hammering. While you're at it, you spend a good 10 minutes inside your head railing against him. You have a complete conversation, telling him exactly what you would like to say to him in person.

Does that make you feel better? Probably not. And on top of all that, you've wasted 10 minutes of your life talking to no one. And then before you know it, here comes another one. "That crazy Cousin Sally better not call to ask if I've heard about the party ..." and you're off for another 10 minutes talking in your head.

We call that "giving someone a piece of our mind." But it's a waste of your time, energy, and health. Oh sure, it feels good to rant, but it gets you nowhere closer to releasing your anger/disappointment/frustration. Your mind is too precious to give away like that, wasting your potential on something (Uncle Joe) you have no control over.

What works a whole lot better is facing the *real* issue—how earlier in your life Uncle Joe hurt you. Now you're on to something you *do* have control over. Only then can you ever let it go. Uncle Joe was just a messenger. He was offering the message of freeing you from the bondage of self.

"The ideal of man is to be a revelation himself, clearly to recognize himself as a manifestation of God."
~ Baal Shem Tov

CASE STUDY

Have you ever felt inundated by stress or messed up at work? Of course you have. We all have. And if you're like a most people early in their journey toward a full and rich life, you probably played the blame game in your mind, with others or with superiors.

But it doesn't have to be this way.

Let me share an example of someone who chose instead to face the issues going on inside her.

Susie is a director in a large firm and manages a team of six. She came to me when she messed up on a very important project. It became clear this error was going to cost the company a serious amount of delay, time and money. Keep in mind Susie is a very smart and competent person. When we started to discuss this situation, her first words were, "I didn't get the numbers." She was playing the blame game. Susie, being a self-aware professional and all-round fantastic person, looked me right in the eye when I asked, "Can I make a suggestion?" She nodded. "Let's clear some energy here by just understanding what was going on for you at the moment when you realized there was a screw up."

For someone who had a hard time taking criticism, this was tough for Susie, but we did a quick session. It would not take that long for her to recognize that she was feeling scared and nervous about her position with the company because of this screw-up. I helped her to release this fear. Then I asked her a simple question: "Do you feel a little freer?"

"Absolutely," she said.

"Okay, so what's your next step? Close your eyes and just think about what your next step is."

All of a sudden, a big smile creased her face. She had a solution for how to re-vamp and fix the issue that was causing this problem. Lo and behold, she was even able to repair the situation. As a result, her superior saw her as a hero because although she'd made mistakes, she took ownership and said, "I honestly screwed up." Through quiet and clarity, she not only addressed the issue openly, she found a better outcome that saved the company time and money!

I keep saying to clients and now you: "Become Free and Prosper."

Susie recognized and learned about the biology of herself. If you'd like to explore this more, check out Dr. Bruce Lipton's

The Biology of Belief, one of the excellent books I recommend from my top 10 list in the back of this book.

NEXT STEP

Here's a simple exercise. Make a list of five people at work who either rub you the wrong way, you've had a tiff with, or you simply don't like. Write down what the circumstances were around that. They left you out of the meeting, they dissed your report, they made fun of your new haircut... whatever the case may be.

As we go on this exploratory journey, I want you to ask yourself what gave you reason to feel uncomfortable around this person. You've already listed your reasons above, but now I don't want you to point your finger at them, as juicy as that can feel. I just want you to get clear on the feelings that made you withdraw from those five people.

In the back of this book, you'll find a Feelings Inventory from the Center for Nonviolent Communication. Look over it and find the feelings you have with these people. Don't just say so-and-so is a putz. Use this list to help you dig down for deeper feelings. I hope by the end of this book, you will get clear on these feelings—and feel freer. This is an ongoing exercise you can use to explore your thinking and learn the language of your inner life.

SELF-DISCOVERY STEP #2: The truth will set you free.

Now I want to focus on what you *do* have control over.

Beyond the preprogramming, you have a lot of free will. And a lifetime of experiences—from childhood to adult years right on up to today. Through those experiences, you've developed a lot of conditioning that affects your day-to-day life (often way beyond the scope of the initial situation).

Sometimes that's good stuff, like when you were a very young child—maybe 3 years old—and you experienced unconditional hugs and kisses from Grandma. Every time you saw her, she made you feel loved, acknowledged and happy inside.

Fast forward to today. You're watching TV and see a commercial with a loving grandmother baking cookies. (Advertisers love to play on our subconscious.) A warm feeling fills you. It's not that pretend grandmother on the TV who's creating that feeling. It comes from your subconscious, from experiences so early you don't consciously remember them.

Or maybe you're food shopping, and you head down the cookie aisle. Lo and behold, you see chocolate chip cookies, and you reach for them without thinking. Deep down your subconscious is recalling those times when Grandma baked them for you. Again, that's the good kind of conditioning (assuming you're not eating *too many* cookies!).

But what about the not-so-good conditioning?

Case in point: Writing this book I experienced writer's block. Thanks to years of working on my stuff, I knew the problem wasn't just about this project. I did some deep digging and found a blockage with origins in my childhood. I went to see a hypnotherapist, Danna Pycher, who helped me discover that I was turned away from a private school because the admissions person told my parents I would not be able to handle a dual curriculum. Even though I never realized it before, I uncovered how over the years I never felt good enough, smart enough or capable enough. That drove me to over-compensate, which led to my becoming very successful financially— but oh so very unhappy. Without realizing it, all those subconscious thoughts were like driving with a...

Windshield Covered with Mud.

Driving through life, your windshield has protected you from being hit by all the insects (life's pain and problems) that come your way. That's the good news. Trouble is, your windshield wipers stopped working a while ago from non-use and faulty maintenance. As a result, your windshield is cover with splats of dead bugs—giving you a dirty and encrusted view of life. Talk about a driving hazard! How the heck could you ever end up where you want to go when you're driving in fear of the next bug about to hit? Not to mention that you can't see where you're going. You're driving blind!

After working with Danna, I realized I needed help clearing up this mess. It took hard work and support from people who have been down this road before. Slowly, I was able to clean off those nasty splats and see more clearly.

NEXT STEP

Don't take my word for it. Investigate for yourself. Close your eyes and travel back in time. Share your pain with a good friend, talk to a therapist, write about it. To help you get started, simply write down the concepts and Next Steps you've read in this book so far. Grab a piece of paper and pen or a special notebook—doesn't matter. Just the act of writing these concepts will make them more a part of your life. Go through the introduction and first two chapters and list all the ideas mentioned there. Then write about how your life resonates with these ideas.

SELF-DISCOVERY STEP #3: Your past isn't your future.

Guess what? Even after you clear your windshield, the bugs keep coming. That doesn't change. What *does* change is your ability to see the bugs coming. That awareness means you get better at using your windshield wipers and other tools to debug your life.

But this requires a shift in direction. Remember how I talked about our pre-installed systems that automatically keep us safe and functioning? They're great, but they can make us lazy. They work so well—at certain levels—that we're lulled into riding through life, going wherever it takes us.

That mindset often gets passed down generation after

generation. As a result, you were probably never taught how to fully function in your life.

Let me repeat that—you were never taught how to fully function in your life. Which begs the questions:

1. How can you expect to drive your life if you've never been taught how?

2. How can you get to where you want to go?

It's like you bought a car but never took driver's ed. Oh, the accidents that causes! So think of this book as a driver's manual. And don't worry that you're not a good driver—yet. You can start the journey wherever you are. As you gain knowledge of where you're going and how you're going to get there, you will naturally start driving with more focus.

Slowly, I was able to clean off those nasty splats and see more clearly.

With new perception (windshield) and self-discovery (windshield wipers) you can start driving better right *now*. Step one is seeing that you have a windshield covered in crud (acceptance), but that was your past (letting go). As you clear your windshield (getting at the truth), you'll begin to see the magnificent, beautiful world all around you. And the truth will set you free.

NEXT STEP

Get to know yourself. It's beyond of the scope of this book to explore all the ways you can do that, but start investigating techniques such as: 1) meditation, 2) hypnotherapy, 3) conscious introspection, 4) good books (see suggested reading in the back of this book, 5) group or individual therapy and so on. Find methods that work for you. And I urge you to try journaling… it's worked wonders for me. (See "Take A Break")

2% FREER TAKEAWAYS:

1.   **Discover what is really driving your life.** Get to know yourself and where you want to go. When you uncover obstacles in your path, study them and then switch gears to get back on track.

2.   **Get help, if necessary, to dig a little deeper.** Open up to the idea of getting help from hypnotherapists, therapists, Rabbis, mentors, books—whatever approach resonates with you.

3.   **Debug your life.** Keep cleaning off residual gunk that could be obstructing your vision and your dreams. It's a lifelong task (but gets easier with practice).

TAKE A BREAK
JOURNALING

Journal writing. I know you've heard of it, but like most folks, you've probably never done it with any regularity. Trust me, it's a great way to get at what's driving your life.

For this practice, handwriting is better than typing, so grab a piece of paper or a notebook or even one of those fancy blank books—whatever works for you—and spend 20 minutes writing down what's on your mind. Perhaps you want to write about your windshield and all those bugs.

What are they? Where did they come from? How can you get your wipers working again?

Write about uncomfortable feelings, unpleasant sensations, unfriendly experiences that lead to resentment, lack, fear, anguish and detachment. What is making you feel disconnected, disturbed, perturbed, rattled, troubled, turbulent? Whatever it is, it's okay. Just uncover what it is and where it came from. Later we'll explore what to do with that information.

Have some fun with journaling. Need more prompts? Here are 10 more to get you rolling:

1. What one action do you regret from your past?

2. What one action do you regret *not doing* in your past?

3. Complete this sentence: I got to where I am now because ...

4. I would have gotten to a good place sooner if my parents ... OK, are you doing those things for yourself now?

5. What are your core values? What in your past helped you establish them?

6. What drives you and how did you come by that?

7. What can you learn from your biggest mistakes? Were there any silver linings?

8. If you could talk to your child/teenager self, what would you say?

9. How have you changed in the past five years? Why did you change?

10. What do you need more of/less of in your life?

Journaling allows you to self-reflect and relieve stress. It also improves your memory and awakens creativity. Give it a try!

3% FREER:
WHERE CAN YOU
FIND ANSWERS?

We're always looking for answers, though too often we're looking in the wrong places. Your best place to start is inside you. Living a freer life is an inside job.

I heard a legend that is worth repeating. As the story goes, God was creating the world and when he came to man, he contemplated where to put the key to man's happiness and joy. So he went to his angels and posed the question. One said put it on the highest, coldest, most difficult and dangerous mountain to reach.

God thought for a moment and said, "Nope, that won't work. I'm creating man to be smart, and he will surely figure out how to climb that mountain to find it."

Another angel said hide it in the deepest darkest depths of the ocean where only the fiercest of creatures live—somewhere surely man would never venture. God contemplated this suggestion and after a few moments said, "No, that won't do, as I'm creating man to be very brave and imaginative, and he will surely use that to find the key there."

Then God's most trusted angel shot up and suggested putting it on the farthest planet in the universe where man could never go. God contemplated this suggestion and quickly said, "No shot! Man is cunning and brilliant. Someday he will devise and build an apparatus that will take him there to locate the key."

God himself turned inward and contemplated deeply on this problem, as he did not want man to find the key so easily that it would lose its meaning and importance. Soon God smiled his most joyous smile and said to his angels, "I have it! I know where to hide the key to man's happiness and joy. I will hide the key inside him, as man will never know to look there. Only if he wants to truly and honestly know happiness and joy will he venture on this most important journey of his existence."

On a more earthly plane, let's consider Joey, who couldn't hold down a job, struggled with his weight and went to the doctor almost every week. His relationship with his mother-in-law, Maureen, grew so strained that when she called to talk to her daughter, she wouldn't say hello when Joey answered—just, "May I speak to Susie?" It bothered him to no end that she'd never ask how he was doing or make any effort to hide her contempt for him. During one session, I asked him a couple of questions:

1.   Has your mother-in-law ever said anything that upset you?

2.   Will your mother-in-law ever say anything in the future that will upset you?

When he answered yes to both questions, I asked why he still got upset every time, expecting a different outcome. I suggested he try to accept the fact that Maureen would never change.

His face turned beet red as he shouted his response: "ARE YOU TELLING ME JUST TO ACCEPT HER? Jeff, if you think I will ever, ever do that, you are out of your mind."

To which I answered, "Then Joey, Maureen controls your life."

You see, it's not the outside events that mold us. It's our *reaction* to the outside world that defines the quality of our lives. Each and every one of us is 100% responsible for the quality of our lives. Your job is to work on becoming aware (no matter how painful) of what energies are being kicked up inside you. As you become familiar with that and learn its language (the inner voice), you can gain the power to free yourself.

That's why I call it an inside job.

The space between your outside and inside world is where the juice lies.

DIGGING DEEPER #1: Stop pointing to the events of your life and blaming them for the quality of your life or letting them diminish who you are today.

It's not what happens to you in the outside world that determines the quality of your life, but rather what's going on inside you. Viktor Frankl, the author of *Man's Search for Meaning*, wrote that book after experiencing the Holocaust in the concentration camps. No human being should ever experience the things he witnessed, but in spite of his outside world, he had the strength to find meaning in his life. The wisdom he shares in *Man's Search for Meaning* (and other books) has made a profound contribution to the world and helped millions of people.

Frankl wrote that between stimulus and response, there is a space, and in that space lies the power to choose your response. Unlike Darwin—the battle of you against the world or, put another way, the fight, flight, or freeze response—you can tap into what is going on inside and change your world. Again, it's not the outside events that mold us. It's our reaction to them that matters.

Consider Maurice, a man in his late fifties. While he's quite accomplished, he's totally disorganized. A man of industry, he just couldn't seem to get to anything done on his to-do list. He reached out to me and asked, "Can you get me more organized? That's my problem."

It quickly became evident to me that no amount of apps, to-do lists, journals, or any kind of fantastic power notebooks were going to help him. The problem was what was going on inside him. Something had knocked him off his game and was blocking him from getting organized.

"Maurice," I said. "Let's be clear. This is an inside job."

He looked at me, perplexed. "What do you mean?"

"The issue is not that you're disorganized. You're disorganized because of what's going on inside you. And the reason I know something else is going on is that getting organized is not that complicated. Right? Pen, paper, lists—done. But your inability to get through your to-do list and address things has its roots somewhere inside your soul."

Through our discussions that followed, it became evident that in his family, one of his brothers was the taskmaster and a very accomplished executor who got stuff done. In comparison, my client felt "less than." He felt less confident and insecure, which in turn affected his life in many ways. Instead of looking directly at his feelings of inability, he chose a variety of distractions to soothe and distract him.

Keep in mind Maurice is very wealthy, an amazing relationship guy and someone with the ability to see the big picture. And yet this issue was nibbling away at him.

Once he was able to address this and get clear about what was going on inside him, he could see that the issue wasn't about to-do lists. It was what was *blocking* him from executing them, that is, his feelings of inadequacy around the family dynamics, his brother in particular. As he learned to release these feelings, i.e., freeing himself, he did go through some painful realizations. But before long, he began to fly as he got more and more stuff done.

He faced the facts about feeling inferior to his brother. Once he was able to release all that—first to recognize it, see it, then release it—he became an efficient executer. Instead of blaming the distractions or life itself for why he wasn't getting organized, he cleared much of the mud off his windshield and could travel his life with more clarity.

DIGGING DEEPER #2: Start taking responsibility for your reactions to the outside world by simply observing them.

Watch your life without judgment. Be a witness to what's going on outside and inside. And pay extra attention to your five senses. Early on, they used to be foremost in our brains for our survival—to ward off saber-toothed tigers or find food to sustain our bodies—as we'd see, hear, smell, taste, feel the world around us. We'd feel wind move through the bush and smell the danger or pleasure it carried. We'd watch and listen carefully about what lay ahead. We were one with our senses.

But today, our senses are mostly for pleasure—beautiful bouquets of colorful flowers, sumptuous aromas from a favorite restaurant, soft cashmere against our skin. Because we aren't hunting for food and shelter, we are detached from our senses, which keeps us from living a fuller, more enjoyable life. Modern science has progressed so much that we can get by without sensing much of anything.

Today, we've become thinking machines on autopilot.

Instead, we spend our time thinking, thinking, thinking. Thinking about the future. Thinking about the past. Thinking about how much money we need. Thinking about whether that important deal will go through. Thinking about going home for the holidays, when everyone will ask why we're not married yet. Today, we're thinking machines on autopilot. Even our cars are becoming self-driving, detaching us further from our self.

I'm advocating that we reawaken our senses to assist in dealing with that saber-toothed tiger. Yes, it actually does still exist, except now it lives in our mind, a.k.a. the *Yetzer Hara* — a predator looking for prey — be it a hated boss, a former friend, a get-rich-quick transaction.

Used properly, our senses are saber-toothed tiger tamers.

One of those inside-job tigers might be your insurance company, which just notified you they will not pay the money you were counting on. That triggers worry. Then you start beating up yourself (and others): "I should never have listened to my Cousin Bob; he's a moron."

See how fast everything turns to blame—in the outside world? But that just delays your ability to get free. Instead, take a deep breath and ask yourself, "What is it that I'm feeling about this situation?" That's the language you need to learn.

NEXT STEP

Sit back, take a few deep breaths and tap into what's going on inside. Pay attention to what you're feeling, hearing, sensing. When you're finished, jot down in a journal what you experienced.

DIGGING DEEPER #3: Stop thinking!

That's right. Just stop. Sit for a moment and bask in the quiet. Smell the tang of the ocean. Hear the chatter of the birds. Feel the warmth of the sun. Even that lawnmower in the distance sounds melodic. To simply sit like that and nonjudgmentally observe, what a beautiful thing!

Now I suggest you stop reading this book and close your eyes for a minute. Just 60 seconds to unconditionally pay attention. OK, go for it.

How was that?

Did you hear some noises from the street? Some music, birds, your stomach growling? To hear *today* is a magnificent thing. When we tap into our senses and use them properly, we gain an extra level of appreciation, love and enjoyment of life, living it in the moment. Keep at it, every day. Along the way, you will learn how your emotions talk to you. You'll start to better sense your energy field, whether you're angry or upset or happy.

You are the experiencer, experiencing life.

Next time something triggers a negative reaction in you, choose your action from a higher level. Like when someone cuts you off in traffic. Sure, it's easy to honk your horn and shout obscenities, but instead, try taking a pause. Relax. Release. Let it go. Maybe that person has a sick dog she's taking to the vet. Maybe she needs to pick up her kids. Or maybe not. It doesn't matter. What matters is that you chose to come from a giving place.

NEXT STEP

Spend more time enjoying your senses. Listen to the information that's being communicated between your outside and inside worlds, because, as we'll discuss next, that's where the music is made.

DIGGING DEEPER #4: Make music.

Let's talk about the way music is made, i.e., how sounds evolve into beauty.

Vivaldi, the Beatles, the Boss—doesn't matter the style—all the great and not-so-great composers know that music happens in the pause. Think of it this way: if you were playing the piano and you held your finger down on a note for five minutes without taking your finger off, would you call that music? No, of course not, because that's just noise. But once you take your finger off the key and put it back down, music is made. Again, music is made in the space between the notes. Without the space (pause) there would be no "Four Seasons," "I Want to Hold Your Hand" or "Born in the USA." No one would ever listen to a song if not for the pause between the notes.

So if music is made between the notes, then we can also say that the music of your life is shaped in the pauses *between* the sounds and actions. You have a built-in, music-making, freedom-generating machine right inside you. It's lying dormant because no one taught you that it's there, why it's there or how to use it! Well, it's time to awaken this gift—the best gift you ever received!

Try this exercise: Listen to some music without judgment, anger or fear. Hear the notes—and the space between the notes. Really get in touch with the music and let the music sweep over you. I promise you, it will set you free.

The (inner) truth will set you free.

Same with your life. Take the time to listen to your thoughts without judgment, anger or fear. You'll find the sweet spot for freedom lies in developing the space (the pause) between stimulus (the outside world) and your response (your inside world).

Now, let's test this on the highway. A truck gets on your tail, headlights flashing in your rearview mirror. He means business. That driver and his truck, the saber-toothed tiger. They've just taken away your freedom, and you're not happy about it.

But not so fast. The reality is that driver is simply driving. (Not very courteously, but still, he's just driving.) The real saber-toothed tiger lives inside your head. Learn this and set yourself free. Sure, this takes practice, but it's a beautiful thing to learn. (Of course, don't close your eyes while driving!)

The first chance you get:

1. Take a deep breath and

2. Communicate with your senses, which are

3. Sending signals to your mind, which is

4. Communicating with your emotions and your heart center.

This is the music of your life.

NEXT STEP

Slow down and get to know yourself. There are all kinds of beautiful, valuable things nestled inside that mechanical mechanism known as *you*. Take your time. Practice, practice, practice. One day at a time through your senses, you'll learn the language—and music—of your emotions and your mind.

DIGGING DEEPER #5: Listen and learn to interpret your inner messages correctly.

Wake up and pay attention to your beautiful life because it is a gift you get to unwrap again and again for the rest of your days. I won't kid you, sometimes the gifts come in odd wrapping paper—or with sour notes—but they're still valuable gifts.

Like Rob, a client I worked with who called me from his car after visiting his grown daughter and grandchild, Bella. "Jeff, I'm so mad at my daughter. She started yelling at me, and her husband just stood there and didn't say a word to help. She told me I'd never be in Bella's life. I never want to go back, and I don't want to do this anymore."

I let him blow off steam, but eventually things quieted down, and we got centered. In the pause between the notes, I asked Rob what he was feeling.

At first, he asked what I meant, but I knew that deep down he already knew. I wanted him to look straight into the eyes of that saber-toothed tiger inside his mind. Yes, I understood it was upsetting to feel unwelcomed at his own daughter's house, but the feeling inside him was what I was after. Slowly, he rose from his lower self (where all the yelling was coming from) to his higher self and got clear. I listened and let him talk. I wanted him to know I was hearing him.

I asked again. "Rob, what were you feeling back there at your daughter's house? What was going on for you?"

After a long pause, he answered, "I felt weak. I felt like a failure as a father."

"Bada bing, bada boom, my friend," I said. "There you go. And congratulations."

I want you to learn how to get at the real issues that keep happiness at bay. The world is there for you to enjoy. Too often we are sitting in our car, bracing for impact. Can I pay that bill? Is my boss mad at me? Why won't my friend answer her phone?

Now, don't get me wrong. Life happens. It throws up tests. But we can get too strapped in, anticipating trouble around every corner, waiting for impact. My hope is for you to start to unbuckle those straps because life is a beautiful ride and yes, it's important to wear a seatbelt, but not every day, 24/7 at work or on the phone or riding the train home. When we're all strapped in, we are releasing tremendous amounts of survival juices called cortisol adrenaline, among others, that are making our lives miserable. Let's change that!

NEXT STEP

Take time to unstrap yourself and live fuller and freer. Like Rob, delve into what you are truly feeling, not just the surface stuff. Write it down—it's gold.

3% FREER TAKEAWAYS:

1. **Make room for truly experiencing life.** Open up to your senses. Feel, smell, taste, see and hear life around you. Then go deeper within to find the messages these senses are giving you.

2. **Stop thinking so much.** Stop thinking so much and find gratitude through speech, prayer, observation and acceptance. Take it one day at a time. Leave behind the turmoil of the past and relinquish the unknown of the future. Spend time in the now and cherish the beauty of life as it is today.

3. **Make friends with the saber-toothed tiger in your mind.** Of course this takes work. It takes practice, but it's a beautiful thing to learn. And it will set you free.

4% FREER:
WHICH CAME FIRST:
THE CHICKEN OR THE
EGG?

We've been asking that metaphorical question for ages, but I think we got the question wrong. We forgot about the shell. *That's* what came first.

For your first nine months of existence, the shell was a physical one that protected you. Then you were born. That's when the invisible shell began to form, a shell that stays with you for the rest of your life. To be sure, the shell offers some important protection. It keeps you safe and gives you a thicker skin for what life throws at you.

But the shell can also work against you—causing unhealthy detachment that leads to unhealthy behavior. I want to spend an entire chapter with this concept because it is so important to your becoming a truly free spiritual being.

The key to your freedom—that is, living shell-less—lies within *you*.

AWESOME ANSWER #1: Why do we need a shell?

Moments before you were conceived, there was a warm, nurturing space waiting for your arrival where you would be safe and protected from the outside world while you grew into more than just primordial ooze. You hung out in this safe space, protected by your personal custom shell (called an amniotic sac) during those formative months.

And boy was life good! You had no idea how good it was because the shell kept you in a state of health and wellbeing. As you had no other point of reference to compare it to, you just assumed that was the way life would always be.

Then your shell broke one physically painful day for you and that nice woman caring for you (whose water just broke). *Hey, wait a minute*, you thought, *I want my protective shell back!* In fact, you wanted it so badly that with the help of that women you squished and squirmed, squeezing your way through a dark, tight passageway.

But when you finally broke free, you discovered your shell was nowhere to be found. You did what most folks do when they experience great loss: You wailed like a freight train!

For the next six months, your days were filled with sleeping, eating and pooping. You were just *being*. Then you added a few more body movements like crawling and putting everything you could find into your mouth. Around 12 months, walking came into play and your discovery phase accelerated into high gear for another 12 months. You were living a wonderfully shell-less existence. Life was not just good; it was super-luscious great! Of course, you don't remember all this, but to confirm my point, just look at an 18-month-old child playing with an old piece of crumpled paper. Joy incarnate.

AWESOME ANSWER #2: When does the invisible shell form?

Around 2 years of age, a new shell is formed. It's different from the one that protected you during your first nine months, which was physical and tangible. This new shell can't be seen or felt, yet it has a strong protective power over you. Wherever you go, it's the lens through which you take in the world around you. It manifested with the aid of your emotions, both happy and fearful. Like the feeling you had while hugging your best toy or playing freely in snow for the first time or getting kissed and tickled by your parents until you burst open with joy. There were also those times when your mind created sadness over not being able to find that toy truck you loved so much or when your parents told you no.

For each of us the factors that went into creating our shell are varied and plentiful. Your parents, your experiences, your society, your physical environment and so on all contributed to it. Basically everything you thought, felt or experienced went into your shell. Today you feel it inside you with all the dos and don'ts, the yeses and noes, the happy and not so happy thoughts, feelings and experiences.

One early example might be a day you don't even remember but it was an important day, nevertheless. You're 2 years old and playing with your favorite toy. Your toy gets taken away and all hell breaks loose as you start to scream at the top of your lungs, "MINE, MINE, MINE." You're thinking, "My world is ending! My toy being taken way = I lose everything I love = My life is over!" Deep inside you a tiny microscopic piece of a shell is born.

Of course, you get over this incident in mere minutes, but this experience—plus thousands like it—contribute to your shell. Like when you were 5 years old and you touched the electrical socket and got scolded. Or when you were 10 years old and a group of friends went to play without you. Or when you rode a two-wheeler for the very first time and felt exhilarated— until you fell down.

Fast forward to age 15. Oh boy, what an age for heavy shelling! How about the first time you experienced a kiss with someone special to you. And then later, when you got dumped by that same person? Or just dealing with teenage angst and gangliness.

As the shell forms, we begin to react to our world from the inside of our shell fragments (blockages). Some areas of our shell are thicker and some places are more porous, depending on the experiences we've had.

Being free lets your present self experience the world.

AWESOME ANSWER #3: How does the shell work?

The shell within is very similar to the membrane of a cell in biology: opening and closing, letting in good nutrients and letting out waste. It works beautifully for us physically. Not so pretty emotionally.

Emotionally, we think we need our shell to protect us from bad experiences and bad people. Our information machine (the mind) through our interpreter (our shell filter/mind membrane) translates this stuff, but too often it gets the words wrong and skews the message. We hold onto large amounts of this crap that in turn runs and ruins our life. Some of it is for good, like not touching a hot stove. Most of it is unhelpful in getting free, especially since most of us don't even know our shell is there. We keep pointing to the cause, i.e., the outside world, but as we learned in the last chapter, it's really an inside job.

A lot of life's events are minor—and yet they leave a major imprint inside that stays with you for years and years to come. All of these thoughts, emotions and experiences play a large part in who you become and how you interact with your life. That can be good or bad. Good for experiencing love and really bad for forgiving and forgetting.

Some people have a very, very hard exterior shell, so hard they cannot even see outside their shell. As time goes by they become harder and harder. The shell is so thick, so hard, so familiar that all they can do is blame everything and everyone for what happened in the past. A lot of people, and it could be you at times, live too much in the past.

Jill, a distant relative who lives on the west coast, is the perfect example of someone who lives her life looking totally in her rearview mirror. As the years passed, she became more and more difficult to talk to and reason with. Whenever we'd talk, she'd bring up the past saying things like, "Remember what so and so said or did?" Her present reality is totally viewed through the lens of her past. That means no person in her life ever has a chance of redemption or forgiveness because she keeps looking at past experiences in order to justify her actions in the present day.

As time went by, more and more family members were no longer communicating with her because all she did was blame something that happened 20, 30, 40 years ago for what was not going right in her life today. She is too busy being invested in the blame game because her windshield was caked in thick mud that was hardened to the point of emotional steel.

Her life was like driving while looking only in the rearview mirror. As her car moved, because life will continue, she kept hitting potholes and stuff in the road because she couldn't see where she was going. Then, of course, she'd turn and look at her past and blame the mud on both her back window and the windshield!

"Well, this person took this advantage, or this was really that, and I was left out of that," or whatever was necessary to continually perfect the blame game.

Don't go down that road! Looking in the rearview mirror is only helpful when you are consciously coming to terms with your past. But for many people like Jill, looking in the rearview mirror gives them permission to not take ownership and just blame. I hope you've already decided not to be a blamer. Turn around, clean your windshield, drive forward. Life is so beautiful right in front of you.

AWESOME ANSWER #4: How is my shell different from someone else's shell?

Depending on a myriad of factors and experiences, you developed a soft, medium, hard or titanium shell. Or possibly a combination shell. For instance, your shell could be a titanium protective barrier that doesn't allow anyone to get close to you, but it's soft and porous when a friend is in need.

How all these shell-creating incidents manifest into our existence is different for each of us. Take someone you might know who believes people are not to be trusted. Chances are this person's life events (or possibly one major experience) made such a strong impression deep inside that they became a very guarded individual. Or consider my life. I remember when I was about 10 years old my reading grade was in the dumpster, and naturally, my mother wanted me to improve. So one day after she expressed her concern, I found her in her bedroom and said, "Hey, Mom. I'm reading a lot more. I'm reading comic books."

"Oh, Jeffrey," she said dismissively, "comic books aren't really reading."

I was crushed. Almost five decades later, I still remember the exact location where I was standing in her room while she was at her makeup table. It was a small incident—but made a major impact on my shell. Let me add that I don't hold this against my mother. She is a loving and caring mom who was just doing the best she could at that moment. But let me tell you, after that event, books and I did not have a great relationship for a very, very long time.

Let's go back in time again. As you grew up you might have been taught "this is what boys do, and this is what girls do." Or "black people do this, and white people do that." Or any variation on this theme, and believe me, there are a million of them. We are exposed to so much just from the media. We see commercials that say eat this and you'll grow strong; play with this toy and you'll be happy; wear these clothes and you'll be cool and have tons of friends as well as be a great dancer! The messages we see and hear from advertisers are daunting and confusing. And as a young child we soak them up and often get swept away into believing what we see and hear as the truth.

How does this relate to shell formation? Well, let's say you watched a commercial for a toy and believed it would make you happy. But your parents said it was a foolish toy or maybe they wouldn't or couldn't buy it for you. That experience, although not profound, stirs emotions that affect your shell.

"Let me out ... I want to breathe in some freedom!"

AWESOME ANSWER #5: What's so wrong with a protective shell?

We walk around life carrying what we believe is our precious shell, believing this is who we truly are or who we think we're supposed to be. But here's the kicker: Not only does our shell skew who we really are, but it also encourages us to seek out experiences, places and people, mostly unconsciously, that *actually make our shell thicker!*

In some cases, we guard and protect our shell with great zeal because we fear breaking it is just too much to bear; that's when our protecting manifests into an addiction. We're too fearful of anyone (mostly ourselves) seeing inside our shell because very deep down we might feel worthless, empty and scared. It's just too frightening to face.

That fear can be so great that we avoid looking inside and choose to self-medicate with drugs (legal and illegal), get into abusive relationships, act out sexually, hurt ourselves physically, binge eat or the opposite. All this just to avoid looking inside our shell, because we perceive it as too painful. We think protecting our shell is way easier than looking inside.

We may go on a career path that doesn't suit us, just because we were never taught, shown or encouraged to go inside, which leads us to choosing colleges for the wrong reasons. All to protect our shell. Sometimes we excessively focus on material objects to keep our shell safe, warm and protected so that someday, we hope and pray, it will hatch into the life we've always felt we were supposed to live. We guard our shell for dear life, becoming closed off and angry, when really we are scared to death of our shell cracking.

Through it all, though, deep down your insides are saying, "Get me outta here ... I'm suffocating under all this protecting. Let me out... I want to breathe in some freedom!"

Our job is to accept ourselves and see what's inside. We need to work on it day by day, moment by moment, to let the garbage out. Not all at once, but gradually. We need to make room by letting go and letting in experiences like love, art, air, the moment. We need to allow ourselves to experience and see the good and the beautiful, because it's everywhere.

God has given us our shells in order to protect us. But as we grow, those shells make us uncomfortable. Good! This nudges us toward breaking these bonds and growing. Rabbi Abraham Twerski[AH] in a 90-second video on handling stress (his most popular, with 80 million views) explains how this works.

He was waiting in his dentist's office when he read an article about lobsters and learned they are made of soft tissue confined within a hard shell. As the lobster grows, it experiences pressure and discomfort, confined by its shell. So it goes under a rock, casts off its lobster shell and produces a new one.

"The stimulus for the lobster to be able to grow is to feel uncomfortable," the Rabbi points out and adds. "If lobsters were able to go to a doctor, they would be given a Valium or Percocet and never grow. ... Times of stress are signals for growth. If we use adversity properly, we can grow through adversity."

You can watch the video at https://youtu.be/3aDXM5H-Fuw

Being free lets our present self experience the world. The freer we become, the more we see; and the more we see, the more we create. Working on having a *shell-less* existence allows us to experience life as it is and helps us stop freaking out whenever that saber-toothed tiger starts to growl.

Seven years ago I married Rochelle, the love of my life. When we first married, she'd comment about something that happened, and I'd get upset. Eventually she told me, "You know, Jeff, you need to get a thicker skin. You're just too sensitive."

I went off to contemplate that and came back to her a few days later. "Honey," I said, "I love you, but I don't want a thicker skin. I want to be skinless. I want stuff to come into me and leave. I don't want it to sit inside of me for years. It's that sitting and holding onto stuff that keeps us from being free."

I'd finally come to understand the shell that protected me when I was young had become a prison. And the only way to break out of that jail is to bring awareness and love inside the shell, which weakens it and makes it more porous.

NEXT STEP

As you're able to recognize what's coming up for you when you interact with others, your self-awareness grows. Take your time and be gentle with yourself as you explore, dig and resolve what is holding you back. Your emotional shell will become thinner and more porous—and you will become freer.

4% FREER TAKEAWAYS:

1. Your shell supported you during your formative years.
Early on you needed a shell to protect you. But over the years, an inner shell developed from your experiences—

both good and bad—and it got progressively thicker and thicker. Now it's time to delve deep within to consciously weaken this shell.

2. The shell actually encourages you to seek out experiences that make it thicker! What you thought was protecting you is really protecting itself. Instead, take time to understand why you're doing things—or *not* doing them. Ask yourself if that's the authentic you in the driver's seat or the you hiding inside the shell.

3. Let yourself out of prison. Consciously bring love, self-awareness, long-neglected dreams and creative adventures into your life. They are the key to open the prison door of your shell so that you can live freer.

5% FREER:
READY TO BREAK FREE?

I t's time to move forward even faster now—into fast-lane key concepts. Buckle up!

As mentioned earlier, we are all born with a pre-installed operating system to help us perceive the world around us. This Percept-O-Meter was installed for a good reason: survival. It helped us see and absorb the environment around us so that we weren't eaten by a saber-toothed tiger or didn't starve to death because our mother couldn't feed us.

That's the good part of your Percept-O-Meter. But like many things, there's a downside too. Somewhere along the way in your evolution this meter began to malfunction. All those inevitable hurts, mixed messages from parents and pressures from society began to alter its lens, and you became misdirected, traveling on the wrong highway. Something intended to protect you was now protecting you right into a guarded, caged life by using all kinds of experiences (family, school, society, government) to limit your real purpose.

In other words, this broken Percept-O-Meter began interpreting your outside world through a damaged filter. Consider the way it gives you messages about past events and how awful they were. Or future events and how bad they're going to turn out. You say to yourself, "If Sally shows up at the party, I'm going to be miserable." What? Really? Your Percept-O-Meter is so badly broken that it thinks it can tell you how things will turn out and how you will feel even before they happen! This is crazy talk!

It's time to wake up and see the road in front of you as it *is*—not as you *want* it to be or how you *fear* it is. Let's get started.

REDISCOVER PRESENT-FULLNESS #1: The road is just the road.

Wayne Dyer said a lot of good things, but one of my favorites is: "If you change the way you look at things, the things you look at change." That's what I mean by present-fullness. Present-fullness is the act of being aware of what you're physically experiencing, emotionally feeling and mentally perceiving (a.k.a. thinking). You just need to listen to the real voice inside you, the voice of God.

And yet like most of us, you spend the majority of your life living everywhere but in the present. Or to put it another way, you're driving in all the wrong directions. Now is the time to stop allowing your interpreter (who, by the way, is doing a lousy job) to send you hither and yon. The wiring in its GPS is all screwed up and left you in a state of "aware mess." But you can change that to *awareness*. How? By waking up to your intuition. Sure, it's gotten a little rusty due to lack of use, but you can get to the next level, walking then running, then driving in *your* right direction.

That's all you need to do: wake up your intuition and, in turn, your belief system. Get in the driver's seat because your Percept-O-Meter cannot fix your outside world. Oh sure, it can tinker with it, but those changes are only temporary. Instead, you can learn to make real change in your life, the kind that eventually becomes second nature and makes your life meaningful.

So how do you get free? By being aware of when you're NOT free.

REDISCOVER PRESENT-FULLNESS #2: God instilled us with perception.

Present-fullness gives us a pathway to living in the Land of Now. To see what you see as it is, not as you think you need it to be. Most people are living in the Land of Then by living in "past-fullness." Or they are living in the Land of When, stuck in "future-fullness," which makes us bloated and sick with worry about things in the future, most of which will never happen.

Somewhere deep inside, our spiritual self has the ability to perceive 24 hours a day. That is likely why we're not even aware of it—it's just part of who we are. But it is important to our whole eco-system that we spend much more time consciously getting to know it and working on reactivating it. Otherwise, we're just walking around believing life "is what it is."

Now, in defense of this Percept-O-Meter, it's at the core of all your actions, behaviors and thoughts. Without it you'd be dead in a day. You might walk into traffic without thinking about the consequences. Or drink scalding hot coffee. Or plow into someone jaywalking.

Those are the obvious examples, but what I want you to focus on are the more subtle, personal situations. You likely don't even notice them, but they are controlling your day-to-day life. Like when you see a person who looks like your ex and a reaction flares up. Or you feel dread and worry when you watch a commercial talking about Alzheimer's. Or even something as simple as when your wife forgets to call you back. Without your clear awareness, most of these daily occurrences can and will keep you in an unfulfilled and unhappy state of mind. Zeroing in on these perceptions is the single most important takeaway from reading this book.

Most of our Percept-O-Meters are broken from misuse and a lack of understanding. Because we are too busy trying to fix or blame the outside for our lot in life, we remain unconscious of what is really going on. Our "aware mess" is looking in the wrong direction. And until we start looking in the right direction, our "aware mess" never ends. Trying to fix our outside world only brings more unhappiness and dissatisfaction.

At the root of the cure is understanding that your Percept-O-Meter's filter is there to help you—not hurt you. Your mess has gotten so clogged that you can't see the truth. So first, you need to recognize that you have this filter. I hope by now in this book you can accept that statement.

Your next task is to clear out your filter. As you do, you will begin to see the truth that the events in front of you have nothing to do with you. They are just events that happened in front of you—nothing more, nothing less.

"Hey, wait a minute," you say. "That job I just lost had plenty to do with me!" Or the wife who just left you or the dog who died too young. Yes, they all hurt, and you'll have to deal with that hurt. But they are still just messages, beacons to help you find your freedom. The information is all there for you, like dials on your car. You have all these beautiful gifts that God has given you, and when you can read them correctly, you'll know what to do next.

It's like when you're driving along and hit a pothole. If you're watching the dials properly and not turning your head back and pointing at the pothole to blame it, you can honestly assess what's happening. "Oh, this bump in the road shows me I need to learn or acquire something." Maybe you'll even know right away what that something is. Or maybe it will take some time and contemplation. But remember—that metaphorical pothole is just a message. It is not an indictment of who you truly are.

NEXT STEP

Present-fullness boils down to living in the Land of Now, that is, being here and paying attention. It's a beautiful land filled with spontaneity, enjoyment, textures, senses, visual, internal bliss and loveliness. Present-fullness means you fully taste life, smell it, hear it, touch it, feel it. Practice being present in the fullness of your life.

Before we move on, I want to add one caveat—you don't have to change or fix everything. Most of us have dents in our car, and it still runs just fine. Get to know your dents and decide consciously which ones you can live with. They don't take away from your getting around, and they don't make you less. In fact, some of those dents make you a more well-rounded person with more compassion for others. Learning to accept them is another way to grow.

"If you change the way you look at things, the things you look at change." ~Wayne Dyer

REDISCOVER PRESENT-FULLNESS #4: Get free by being aware of when you're NOT free.

Let me share an example from a client of mine. Jack was getting serious in a relationship with a woman he really liked, and it was going pretty well. During one date, his girlfriend started to ask more questions about him. "I want to know about your past," she said.

A few days after this date, Jack came to me and mentioned he was going to meet her the next day to talk. I could tell there was something else he wanted to share. When I asked about it, he said, "Over the past three days, my mind has been giving me fits. I keep hearing over and over that she's *going to break up with me when she finds out about me.*"

These thoughts had convinced Jack she would leave once she knew more about him. Something he'd tell her would make her think less of him.

Now first, let me tell you something about Jack. He's a divorced community man with a loving family and great friends. He has created six successful businesses across different industries that have made him a millionaire. And as it happens, he experienced a very similar upbringing to most of his community members.

So we sat together and eventually, I said, "Let's get clear, Jack. Let's go back to the moment she asked the question. What were you feeling?"

He became still and answered, "I'm scared of not ever being loved. And I'm frightened she's going to leave me. I really like her."

"Okay, good for you," I said. "Congratulations. Now, why don't you just sit there quietly, do the work that we've spoken about so that you can release this."

After just those few minutes, Jack was able to identify what he was afraid of—that he would never be loved. He could see now that it wasn't her; it wasn't his past. He wasn't blaming anybody, and now that he'd identified the issue, he could release it.

Yes, this work can be uncomfortable, but it's the path to freedom. Jack did the work and released those negative feelings. When he saw how un-free he was in that situation, he was able to lower the intensity level around those feelings from a 10 to a 9, and he became 10% freer.

After the freedom exercise, Jack felt and looked lighter. He smiled and said, "I'm going to tell her whatever she wants to know. I care about her, and I want her to know about my past, and I'll leave it up to powers greater than me as to what she does with this information."

Yet through this process, they actually became closer. She opened up about her past as well. It's a beautiful thing, and now they share closeness, honesty, intimacy—*real* intimacy. I recently heard they're even talking about marriage!

Now it's your turn. In addition to getting still and listening, here are three more steps you can take, starting today:

1. **Let Go and Let God.** Let go of what is blocking you from God, or oneness. This is the beauty of present-fullness. Use it to tap into being in the Land of Now, to free yourself from the interpreter that is translating everything all wrong.

2. **Listen to your *real* voice**—your intuition, that quiet voice within, which is also known as God. God is talking to you 24/7/365. Some people mistakenly believe that the personal mind—"I like, I don't like"—is the real voice. It's not! Please let go of what's giving you spiritual indigestion.

3. **God gave us the ability to free ourselves.** Just like we have the ability to release food we eat through our magnificent biological system, listen for when you have to go to the spiritual bathroom. God wants to help you cleanse the toxins that have built up in your soul from years of not paying attention. You can rid yourself of mental and

spiritual toxins through perception, insight and intuition.

In earlier chapters I talked about driving on the road of life and coming upon a major delay. It's literally messing up your timeline for the day for that all-important appointment or event. It would be easy to get worried and annoyed just because of all that traffic. But we can learn to practice our patience. Instead of screaming, which a lot of people do in the privacy of their cars, you can see the situation as "it is what it is." All the screaming in the world won't move those cars any faster. Relax, then dig a little deeper. This is an opportunity to check in with yourself to see if there's a message waiting for you.

And of course, traffic jams are a metaphor for all kinds of things in your life—waiting to hear from an important client, waiting for your computer to load a document you need, waiting for someone to do what they promised. It could be anything. Work on relaxing, which will help you identify what's going on.

NEXT STEP

Why not play with this concept? Next time something small annoys you—like the internet goes out while you're playing an online game—look inside and honor that you're annoyed. Good for you! You realize you're dealing with an inside job—misery of your own making. Once you've identified the issue and the feelings, let it go. Again, Let Go and Let God. Now, at least you know what's going on. Tell yourself, "I'm just feeling annoyed. I'm going to recognize being annoyed." Gradually, the feeling of being annoyed will drift away with the clouds, and you've learned a beautiful new language—the language of freedom.

5% FREER TAKEAWAYS:

1. The road to freedom is paved with potholes and traffic—and they're all an opportunity for you to practice and work on freedom.

2. Use your intuition and perception to hone in on what you're truly feeling. Honor that and know that you can decide how you want to react and feel.

3. Learn to relax and be patient by seeing your life as it is—and being grateful for it.

6% FREER:
WHERE IS THE BEST PLACE TO LIVE?

It seems magazines and newspaper editors can't get enough of those stories about the best places to live. They take their readers all around the world to different cities and countries in search for the perfect place. Except they've missed the boat. The best place to live is in the pause, the now, where we're fully conscious of what's going on around us.

But what do most of us do? Like those editors, we hop from place to place. We live inside our minds. We hear the interpreter say things like: *When are we getting that order? What are my people up to all day? I'm a shmuck for hiring that idiot! Maybe he's not that bad, but where is the program! Our expenses are through the roof! Why did I take this showroom space! I can't believe my AMEX bill this month! I told my wife to cut the clothes spending! I should cut her limit. NO way can we go on vacation.*

Folks, this is madness. No wonder people jump off bridges! Let's take a look at the *real* best place to live.

Living in the pause is living in reality of *what is*. Not *what was* and not *what will be*. Seeing what is right in front of you and being in the moment gives you a gateway, an opportunity to view life clearly and accept *what is*.

We are usually so busy living in *the then* and *the when* that we find ourselves emotionally drained, in part because we are using valuable energy dwelling on past troubles or anticipating problems yet to come. A sure way to drain your batteries.

By seeing and living in the Land of Now, it becomes so much easier to deal with what comes up. You're no longer dealing with all those "shoulda-wouldas"; you're dealing with *what is*.

Living in the now, being present-full, we create space to experience life at a higher level. Simple things like a sunset, a cup of coffee, or the sounds of birds radiate with joy. Love, hugs and kisses? They explode with new power. In fact, when we live in the now, we're actually creating a tremendous amount of renewable energy for our journey.

The COVID experience was devastating for many. I, as I'm sure you do too, know people who suffered greatly during this dark time.

But for me personally, my awareness of *what is*, i.e., my willingness, my acceptance, my understanding of the reality that was in front of me, actually increased. I was able to extend my reach in helping people by not living in my past. I was able to secure more corporate clients and executives. I opened an office in Brooklyn and improved my relationship with my wife and family. In fact, this book, which had been percolating for some time, was conceived in 2020.

At the same time, my awareness was greatly magnified. We all had to be keenly aware of what we were touching, what we were doing. We paid attention to washing our hands, our breathing, our talking and our doing.

This experience increased my present-fullness practice to a level higher than it had ever been. There were many moments over this past year that were the best of my life. I came to grips with seeing, feeling, experiencing the moment because in the moment, I was fine. Living in *the then* or *the when* would have caused a lot of anxiety, frustration, upset and fear.

"Low self-esteem means that a person is unaware of one's strengths and abilities, and hence underestimates oneself." ~ Rabbi Abraham Twerski[AH']

I want to share two important experiences I had.

1. At one point, I consciously decided to up my dosage of my "Red Pill" prescription. (Remember the movie "The Matrix"? The Red Pill is "reality.") I kept upping my doses of reality and increasing my awareness by meditating, breathing, sensing,

touching and regularly thinking before I spoke.

So far so good.

Then I noticed that my attention to the present moment was so acute that midway through this pandemic and lockdown, I realized my loud inner voice was taking inventory of my wife's actions 24/7. "Why didn't she put the laundry this way? How come she didn't do this or that?"

For a short period of time the voice was non-stop! I must say she was absolutely amazing during the whole time, but it was my inner bully roommate, aka *Yetzer Hara*, that was trying to test our relationship.

Later, I told a friend, "Oh, my goodness, I have been so judgmental for the past two weeks." It really was an eye-opener, and I was able to recognize it and see it for what it was. Because I could have sat there and complained, "Well, you know, she should be ... And she could be ... After all, I always ..." The *Yetzer Hara*/dark energy would have loved that! But no. I needed to listen to the message, and the message was clear.

I sat quietly, did my work and recognized that I was taking her inventory because of my lack. My lack of not being recognized for doing an AMAZING job! (Though my wife *was* complimenting me throughout this time while I was working from home.) I felt I wasn't being appreciated for all that I was doing, and this led me to feeling resentful. Then I got clear on what I needed—to stop taking her inventory and be grateful for the fact that I happened to have the loveliest, most beautiful, magnificent wife on the planet.

But first I needed to release my neediness, my lack of security before I could become free from it. And when I did, I experienced a shift in my work. By recognizing and releasing my lack at home, Hashem was able to open me up to be of more service—and that increased my business.

Living in the pause gives us a gift if we choose to see and accept it. It's the gift of clarity to deal with *what is* and not let it deal us. Can you imagine the fights I could have had with my wife? This stuff causes wars! How many unnecessary arguments could have been avoided for couples and families if they went inside themselves for the answers?

2. When we see *what is* in the moment, everything is much more manageable and potentially transformative. The renewable energy we generate can be channeled into creation, music, art, cooking, friends, and yes, even into cleaning. You become the Picasso of *you*.

During COVID, I wasn't just digging deeper into my thoughts; I was very active in my home. Because I was home more, I started noticing tasks that needed tending. I was excited by all this because I was tapping into the pool of unending renewable energy. What did I create? A storage room for all of our washing stuff underneath the sink and in our laundry area. I started by moving everything out of the space. I studied the problem and looked at all the items that needed to fit in there. I spent time measuring, thinking and planning. Then I went online, bought some storage things, cleaned everything up, and felt extremely accomplished.

I did that all over the home, and I have to say, there are times when I did it a little bit too much. But I can recognize that, and I can laugh at my over-the-top OCD organization, but so what? I was having fun. I was creating, and my wife and I were laughing and loving.

Life loves all of us unconditionally.

Living in the now, we are living from our higher self, which creates opportunity for us to see the forest from a higher perspective. When you see what is, you see the truth. As you've heard me say before, "The truth will set you free." Because it does!

Living in *the then* or *the when* is living from our lower self, living from lack. It's like living and viewing life from a ditch in the road. But if we work on recognizing that when we go into the ditch of *the when* and/or *the then*, there is an opportunity given to free ourselves and lift ourselves to our higher self.

One of my clients said early on in our sessions, "You know, Jeff, you talk about this awareness thing. What happens if I become too aware?"

I took a deep breath and listened to him. When we drilled down and unpacked what he'd shared, it became clear that he was feeling fearful of actually experiencing himself in the moment. I respect that. Not everyone is prepared to live in the now.

Present-fullness does not mean you live in this free, unencumbered nirvana life. It means, for example, that when you need to make a shift, you come to realize that like the lobster, that happens through uncomfortability. I made up that word, because it perfectly describes that feeling of something not feeling quite right. Put another way, you need to see when you're in the ditch and blaming the road, the driver next to you or the weather. Understand your feelings about being in a ditch and listen to your heart (the closest organ to your soul).

BRILLIANT BENEFIT #1: Slow down and smell, taste, feel your life.

Some Jews wear tefillin on their forehead and arm during morning prayers. For those of you not familiar with tefillin, it's a set of small black leather boxes containing scrolls of parchment inscribed with verses from the Torah. One of the primary purposes of putting on tefillin each morning is to sanctify the five senses: sight, hearing, smell, taste and touch.

Rabbi Wagensber explains the importance of the tefillin this way: "The four senses are found on the head: sight, hearing, smell, and taste. The head tefillin, known as *shel-rosh*, has four compatments representing those four senses. And the fifth sense, touch, is found on the hands, which is why the arm tefillin, known as *shel-Yad*, has only one chamber built inside of it. The tefillin are a physical reminder while reading the morning Shema to awaken us to love Hashem through all our senses."

Whether you wear tefillin or not, you can activate your consciousness to pay closer attention to the senses. When you do, life slows down just long enough for you to sense the moment. You pause, and you become more conscious. When you stay present, you become free.

Practice noticing what you're physically sensing and

emotionally feeling. When you pause to do this, you will expose your mind for what it is: just an overworked machine operating 24/7/365. It's time to become aware and shine a bright light into the madness of this mind machine. Pay attention to what it is interpreting and translating. That puts you on the most direct road to Freedom Town.

BRILLIANT BENEFIT #2: Step out of "The Matrix" to see what is ... as it is.

In one of the last scenes in "The Matrix," Neo is lost inside the Matrix and running scared inside his interpreter. He's consumed by fear, doubt and uncertainty. Then he's shot and dies. But a kiss brings him back, which is a metaphor for connection, that all-important aspect in living a rich, full life. He allows himself to be kissed by life because life loves him. That's true for you and me too. Life loves all of us unconditionally. We must work on allowing life to kiss us. Stop turning your cheek away! It's harming your life, and it's disrespectful to God!

After Neo finally wakes up, he is able to see the bullets as they truly are—an illusion inside his mind machine. When he recognizes the illusion, the bullets literally stop mid-air. They have no hold on him whatsoever. They have become powerless. Finally, Neo jumps into his fear (as portrayed by Mr. Smith in the movie) and eradicates it. He is free.

Time to wake up to see, smell, feel the moment in front of you. Witness it—*now*. We spend years in front of the TV and computer, but we need to spend more time with the real moment. Everything in front of you is a gift made for you! Tune into ChannelYou and limit your time on YouTube!

"He who is full of joy is full of love." ~Baal Shem Tov

NEXT STEP

Like the scene in "The Matrix," once you clearly see the "bullets" in your life, you can slow them down too. The bullets are emotionally charged messages that need your attention. When you see them as they are—simply information and data—you can take a big step toward your freedom. Don't let your life play out like a horror movie. Take some time to look closely at your emotionally charged "bullets." What are you giving too much power to? How can you deactivate these powerful weapons that are screwing up your life? Put some time aside to live with this idea and then Let Go, Let God.

BRILLIANT BENEFIT #3: Live in the pause.

The question "How do I live a better, happier more meaningful and productive life?" has been written about and contemplated throughout the ages. And you know what? The answer is quite simple: Live in the pause. Like I mentioned earlier about making music, the pause is an important part of communication. If two people are discussing their feelings about the new coffee bar down the street, and if they proceed to do so by both talking at once or someone talking without taking a break, that would just be noise, certainly not a quality conversation. Only when one person stops talking and lets the other person join in would we call that a conversation.

Well, the same goes for you, inside your own head. Think of all those noisy conversations you have in that mind of yours. It tends to never, ever stop talking. That, in turn, activates your emotions, which activates feelings of shame, guilt, regret, resentment, fear. When you feel this happening, step back and let this episode pass by instead of becoming an actor in it (inside your mind).

I once had a client who was going through a difficult business decision. Day and night, he kept ruminating on making a choice. He was so stuck playing ping-pong inside his mind with the *what ifs* and *what was's* that he missed the opportunity to secure a very lucrative licensing deal.

When we got together, I suggested some tools and techniques to help him put some space between him and his mind. He baulked because his need to feel in control of every business decision was greater than his need to be free. He wasn't ready to let go of that control or to delegate more. He chose to be a prisoner of his thoughts. This is an extreme case but it illustrates how your mind, when left to its own devices, will destroy your life. But when you work on living in the pause, you're creating space inside your mind in between thoughts and reactions, and that space is your path to freedom.

According to Web MD, 75 to 90 percent of all doctor's visits are for stress-related ailments and complaints. Newsflash folks! It's not the stress that is the cause. It is our reaction to it! As Viktor Frankl said, "We can choose our response."

In other words, to get freer, we need to dance in that space where we have stress—like the space between the notes that makes it music. That's where our growth comes from—and our freedom. So next time you're in a hurry and someone is in your way, don't react. Release your anger. If you practice this, I know one day someone will cut in front of you or take forever to get their wallet out to pay, and you'll later tell me you reacted for only one or two seconds. And that your anger drifted off with the notes coming out of your radio.

NEXT STEP

Practice being here and now. You're at a crossroads, and you have the option of going up (high self) or down (lower self). Many people choose the latter and say, "I can't help it; it's just the way I am." But that's a cop out. That is just the way they have decided to be. God gave us free will, also known as the big pause. You can strengthen this free-will muscle. We'll get into that more soon.

6% FREER TAKEAWAYS:

1.   **Be aware of what's on your mind machine.** Listen and decide how you want to participate.

2.   **Take the high road to your high self.** Step back from all the chatter and avoid getting caught up in it.

3.   **To live a joyful existence, you must live in the pauses.** That space is where the beautiful music of your life is made and experienced. Without an active pause muscle, you'll miss out on a life filled with music.

TAKE A BREAK
GRATITUDE

"It is through gratitude for the present moment that the spiritual dimension of life opens up."
~ Eckhart Tolle

Gratitude can change your life. In fact, recent research has determined it can change your brain. People who take just a few moments every day to recount what they're grateful for are happier and healthier.

So why not add a regular gratitude practice to your life? Here's an easy one that takes only 20 minutes.

Sit and get quiet. Then say to yourself, "Thank you, Hashem. Thank you, God, for…" and let your mind fill in anything that comes to you or that you actually see in front of you. The pen you're holding. The book you're reading. Your eyes. "Thank you, God, for the eyes that I can see. Thank you, God, for the breath that I can breathe. Thank you, God, for the coffee I am drinking. Thank you, God, for the chair I am sitting on. Thank you, God, for the sky I see. Thank you, God, for the car I'm in. Thank you, God, for the red light I am seeing. Thank you, God. Thank you. Thank you. Thank you."

Live in gratitude for 20 minutes. I've heard it said, and I'm sure you have too, that when you live in a state of gratitude, you develop an attitude of gratitude that will lift you up and carry you forward. That's actually vibrationally very powerful. Try it … you'll like it!

Consider this gratitude attitude story about David. He had gotten COVID, not too seriously, but as he was recovering a few weeks later, he was excessively concerned that his sense of smell and taste had not come back yet. He was riddled with fear of "then what" and "what if" and borrowing calamities that may or may not happen in the future. He kept saying, "I want it back now!" and living in a tremendous amount of lack and fear.

The reality is he lost his sense of smell and taste. How long would that last? I couldn't answer him. But I did tell him, "Look, David, let me give you this simple exercise. For the next 20 minutes just say thank you to Hashem for everything." David has three beautiful young kids, so I told him, "Just say 'Thank you for the kids. Thank you for my wife. Thank you for the water I'm drinking. Thank you. Thank you. Thank you for my clothes. Thank you. Thank you.' Do this for 20 minutes."

And he did. After just one session, he called me immediately to say, "Jeff, it was amazing. You won't believe what happened!" OK, his sense of smell did not come roaring back (though it finally did a few weeks later), but more importantly, what came to him as he was saying thank you for everything in front of him, his 7-year-old daughter came up to him and said, "Daddy, would you help me with this project?"

She was doing a creative project for a beautiful holiday called Purim, a joyous, magnificent holiday to give thanks, to be grateful for our lives. He was blown away, and told his daughter, "I would love to." For that moment his smell and taste concerns vanished. He was able to experience the moment and the true meaning and mitzvah of Purim, which is all about celebrating our freedom! That is beautifully magical stuff!

"The truly great human beings are those who have opened themselves to the inspiration of something greater than themselves." ~Rabbi Joseph Sacks AH'

7% FREER:
WHAT THE BLEEP IS MY SOUL SAYING?

Your soul is talking to you, and what it has to say is very important. But it can be hard to hear over the noise of your personal mind, a.k.a. *Yetzer Hara.*

The soul's voice is quieter; it's your intuition or God-inside-you voice, a.k.a. Hashem.

They're both part of you, and even the loud voice is there to help you. All that screaming and complaining? Though it can feel very uncomfortable at times, it's trying to get you to listen to the quiet you, the *real* you. That loud voice really does want you to pay attention to the God inside you. But most people, so accustomed to the commotion, hear only the noise.

A PERSONAL CASE STUDY

A client gave me the task of moving an employee to another department. The CEO instructed me to do it, which affected his partner. The affected partner angrily called me and was so unpleasant that I raised my voice and hung up on the guy. I was extremely angry, upset and frustrated. This wasn't my usual way of interacting, and deep down I knew my uncharacteristic behavior needed to be addressed. Oh, but I was having none of that! I got caught up with that loud voice inside *me* and let it rant for a night.

The next morning, the loud voice and bad feelings were still sitting with me. But fortunately, my uncomfortability led me to what needed to be done. I sat and became still, which helped me see clearly what was going on inside me. I quietly asked myself: *What am I feeling about this? Why did I get so upset?*

Honestly, it was hard *not* to be upset. I felt justified resenting the partner I hung up on, but I knew that would be looking in the wrong direction. It took only a few minutes of stillness to identify a feeling of being violated and unappreciated. I knew that was at the core because I thought I had built a really nice relationship with this individual. I was hurt.

I thanked God for giving me this uncomfortable gift and then released it. I had such a strong physical release—it touched my soul so deeply—that I actually coughed throughout this getting-free session.

With this new level of freedom, I was able to have a conversation with the partner. And it was wonderful. I could hear his hurt unconditionally, and as a result, our relationship increased tenfold as I gave him the space to explain where he was coming from.

Let's take a closer look at how this plays out in your life.

"The Gain is in the Pain." ~ Rabbi Jonathan Sacks

INSPIRING INFORMATION #1: Learn your soul's real language.

OK, we've identified the loudmouth, *Yetzer Hara*. And you now know your quiet voice is your intuition, higher self, heart consciousness, a.k.a. God or Hashem.

Due to your life circumstances and a lack of understanding, education and/or other factors, you've probably relinquished your free will, only to find yourself on the road to Unhappy Town, the place where all your dreams are *not* fulfilled. This town is brimming with shops, rides, movie theaters, but they're filled with unhealthy treats and unfulfilling experiences.

Inside of you, quiet and loud are battling it out for your attention. Make no mistake—this is a battle between freedom and slavery, and it's going on inside your mind daily. Like I keep saying, we all spend too much time focusing our energy on the outside in an effort to fix the inside. But by now you know you can't fix the engine (your soul) by giving your car (your life) a new coat of paint. And you can't fix the engine while the car is moving.

Your soul is in constant communication with you. You need to learn its real language. It's the road map to help release you from the bondage of your ego self (*Yetzer Hara*) –, the one that wants you to be a zombie or prisoner.

As you learn how to understand the communication system inside your soul, inside your body, inside your being, you'll be able to unlock the excitement and enthusiasm that's also inside you. And that's when you'll see that you're headed toward freedom.

NEXT STEP

You're the pit crew boss of your car. You hold the key to the repairs and improvements it needs. That's how you finally get to Freedom Town. So take your foot off the gas, slow the car down and start listening to the quiet voice of the engine. It's talking to you!

INSPIRING INFORMATION #2: Now *listen* to your soul.

Each and every day, all day, you need to work on listening to the quiet voice inside your engine. That quiet voice holds your get-out-of-jail-free card. In other words, *you* hold it. It's the key to the cell you've locked yourself into; it's your key to the kingdom. If you can listen to that, you will hear the truth. And at the risk of sounding like a broken record (because this is so important!): "The truth will set you free."

You will learn the truth. You will understand a new, unbelievable foreign language, and you'll be able to explore a new land, a beautiful, magnificent place on planet Earth. It's the land of freedom. The freedom of you!

To make this clearer, let's explore an example of how the outside world can drown out the voice inside your engine and take over your driving. Let's say you went on JDate.com, set up a date, and you're looking forward to it. When you saw her picture and bio, something inside you said, "Yeah, let's take a chance. She's cute, and I feel good about going on this date with Deborah." (So far so good; it seems you were listening to your heart!)

But look out! Here comes your dark ego/*Yetzer Hara* roaring up behind you, unable to resist ruining your fun. As you're preparing for your date, it starts needling you. *What happens if she doesn't look like the picture on JDate.com? What if she's ugly? Or smells bad? What happens if I like her but she doesn't want to go on another date?*

What if, what if, what if! Oh, but there's more: *Maybe she doesn't like short men. Why did I let Judy talk me into doing this? I never liked her taste in women! Then comes the kicker: Well, maybe I should just cancel!*

This is a crazy, crazy way to live; yet so many of us do it, listening to that noisy, loud, broken engine as if it's the truth. And in some ways it is, but not for the reasons we think it is. It does have a purpose—to help propel us on our drive toward freedom—but only when we consciously listen to it.

Another client of mine, Sam, was working at a company for 10 years where he was the righthand man of a very powerful individual. Sam had become an integral part of this man's business, and as a result he was pushed to the limit with tasks to handle. In addition, a tremendous amount of unappreciation, miscommunication, distraction and uncomfortability tainted their work relationship, so much so that Sam was angry each and every day. It became so bad that on many occasions he said he'd be driving home, screaming at the situation going on at work. This was also affecting his wife, his kids, and his health. This stuff spills over to all areas of our lives.

It took several months, but as we worked together, he was able to come to grips with what was going on for himself. He came to see that the boss was just a messenger to help him get free. That boss happened to be a wonderful guy, but he was going through his own stuff. When Sam started to get clear, he was even able to have compassion for his boss.

For years and years, Sam hadn't listened to the real message. He was just screaming at the situation and his circumstances. He felt trapped. When he finally became quiet and started to listen, he could accept himself for what he was. And he was able to release what was holding him back. He no longer was blaming his boss for the potholes in his road. He was able to get free, grow and move on. He moved on to a new position in a much larger company, where he is now helping other people get free. In addition, he's earning five times his previous salary with huge financial gains; his relationship with his wife and kids has never been better; and he wakes up every day with enthusiasm and excitement for what the day has to offer. Sam is living a life beyond his wildest imagination.

NEXT STEP

Learn how to first quiet the ego/*Yetzer Hara* inside of you and raise your awareness of your God-conscious voice. The mere act of working on quieting the noisy engine will automatically allow you to start hearing the intuitive voice.

The way to do this is through meditation or by getting still and grounded on your journey. Stop and listen to the wheels turning on the road, hear the wind, see the trees, notice the other cars, smell your surroundings, sip and actually taste your coffee, look at the clouds, feel the steering wheel in your hands. In other words, be present-full. Live and experience living in the Land of Now, not the Land of Then or When. Start listening to the soundtrack of yourself. It's playing your life, right in front of you—for free! No ticket or subscription needed. I understand why we run from the Land of Now. Michael Singer says it beautifully: "The mind is where the soul goes to hide from the heart." It can be hard, I know. It's a battle in there, but it can and must be won.

"It's during our darkest moments that we must focus to see the light." - Aristotle

INSPIRING INFORMATION #3: God wants to kiss you each and every moment. Don't turn away!

That's right. God wants to kiss you every morning, afternoon and night. Those kisses are packaged in all the beautiful, everyday things. Gifts like a sunrise, laughter, clouds, water, food, aromas, touch and on and on. But too often we are not paying attention. In fact, we turn our cheek when God tries to kiss us.

In the Jewish faith, from the moment we wake up and throughout our day, we are required to say Baracha from **Modeh Ani** (מודה אני) to our last Shema before we sleep.

So many of us say these prayers mindlessly. The purpose of our blessings and prayers lies in our need and desire to give thanks to our creator, Hashem. We must take a pause, slow down if only for a moment to not only say the blessing but to experience that glass of water, that amazing piece of fruit, those precious moments with our family. For me, I see Hashem's physical manifestation of his unconditional love for us in the form of an apple. All we have to do is slow down for a moment to bless and experience its magnificent flavor. Rabbi Avigdor Miller shares this in his profound teachings, which are captured beautifully by Rabbi Dov Keilson in his book *Open Your Eyes: Seeing Hashem Everywhere*.

Our job is to be aware of when God is talking to us, even when sometimes that comes wrapped in pain or discomfort. When you do, you will get to know the warden of your prison cell, who just happens to be... *you*. You will discover the keys to your jail cell are in your pocket. Yeah, that's where the keys are, and guess what? *You* put them there! Get them out and unlock the key to the kingdom that lies within you. Now you can see that I was telling you the truth when I told you that right behind those painful experiences is the best gift of all: freedom.

Each and every day, all day, you need to work on listening to the quiet voice inside your engine.

That's what Alfred did. He worked with a partner who was difficult and abusive. He felt trapped and saw his situation as hopeless. But when he finally got clear on what it is that was going on inside him, when he stopped the blame game, he said,

"I'm taking responsibility for my situation and responsibility for doing something about it."

As a result he was able to free himself from his circumstances and move on. He left his job and ended the relationship with a wife who, though he loved her, was not right for him. Today he has a great relationship with his ex-wife, he built a new business that is thriving, and he's working every day, getting freer.

A note about change: I don't want you to think you only need to work out what's going on inside you so that you can better cope with your life. Compassion and understanding can work wonders, but sometimes you still need to do things differently. The key here is to know *why* you're changing; that is, make a conscious change so you're not running from one mess to another. It's like the difference between driving with a good road map and driving aimlessly.

Folks, this journey is not a one-and-done situation. Life keeps happening, keeps evolving. We're always going to get messages. We're always going to face challenges to get freer and freer. The Creator wants us to be happy, joyous and free. So we get challenges to do just that. The question is, "Are you listening?" Or are you pointing fingers and playing the blame game? The blame game is the easy way out at the moment, but the long-term effects are disastrous.

The blame game is like sitting in the backseat of your car while driving! You can't change the windshield wipers, it's a long stretch to make a left signal or a right signal, and it's impossible to hit the brakes. There's so much noise, you can't even hear the music on the radio. Your life is like the scenery whizzing past your window. You can't experience it because you're too frightened of getting into an accident. Who wouldn't be? You're stuck in the backseat, bracing for impact. Even 10 seatbelts couldn't help you avoid an accident from back there.

So, will you or won't you take ownership for your drive? Would you rather blame someone else (who's not even driving your car!) for the potholes and ditches you land in? Or blame life because your tires keep going flat?

For crying out loud! It's time to get in the front seat! Take ownership for your vehicle and take control of it. Now you can see your dashboard to see if your car's overheating or needs more oil. Maybe your car needs a full-service wash. Give it what it needs to take you on a journey, the likes of which you've never seen before!

When you no longer try to make the outside world fix your inside world, when you take responsibility for your dance with the outside world, then you take the lead. You take ownership of your car and say: "*I'm* going to sit in the driver's seat. *I'm* going to drive." Once you're up front, you'll discover so many opportunities to be free and enjoy the journey.

That is a major point of this book. I have no idea where you have been or where you are going, but I can help you enjoy the ride. Potholes? Get over them! Traffic jams? Don't let them distract you from your life. Can you see it up ahead? It's waiting for you. Right now, in this moment, go ahead and see, smell, taste, hear, feel and experience your life for the magic it is.

NEXT STEP

Don't let the EGO—Edging God Out—run the show. God wants to care of you, just as if you were an infant. Because truth be told, we are all infants in this game of life. Infants trapped in an adult body with so much to learn every day. Turn toward God and take responsibility for your life.

7% FREER TAKEAWAYS:

1. You can learn what your soul is really saying to you— beyond all the chatter and noise of the outside world. Every day, quiet your mind so that you can hear the wisdom your soul wants to share.

2. Once you can hear, pay attention to the soul's messages. It loves you and wants the best for you. Let it guide you toward authentic peace and freedom.

3. As you quiet your mind, you will sense that God is with you, kissing you and caring for you. Don't turn away!

"The mind is where the soul goes
to hide from the heart."
~Michael A. Singer

8% FREER:
WHAT KIND OF GIFT IS *THAT*?

Gifts come in all kinds of wrapping. Gifts from God are often wrapped in ways that make the gift hard to recognize—or something you want to avoid. What I mean is, sometimes they're wrapped in doo-doo. Ugh! Who would want to open a gift like that? Or they come wrapped in an unexpected detour or roadblock.

But that's OK. Some of the best gifts at first seem like misfortune, disappointment, or even despair.

As you make your way through these starts and stops, keep your mind open to what I alluded to earlier: the biology of spirituality. Just like we have a bodily digestive system, we have a spiritual digestive system that requires your attention. Let's dig deeper and fine-tune this process.

It works like this: Life is going along just fine, and then your spiritual ecosystem starts to rumble. It doesn't feel right, but again, this is the gift of uncomfortability. In the past, you probably thought this unease meant something was wrong, or whatever was happening freaked you out so much that you stuffed it somewhere down deep.

But now I invite you to look at it as a message. A gift. Look at your uncomfortability head on and learn to accept what it *is*. Don't fight it. Recognize it and use it. And when you do, you will no longer feel bad when uncomfortable things happen. Oh sure, you may feel ill at ease at first, but not for long. You will start to feel and react differently from how you have in the past.

We've talked about this earlier in the book, but now I want to delve more deeply into this fundamental principle of living 10% freer. It's time to explore more fully how taking responsibility for your life makes your life so much richer.

"You cannot address a problem in your life with the same mind that got you there in the first place." ~ Albert Einstein

REMARKABLE RESULTS #1: Get to know your gunk.

Let's go back to our car metaphor. On this journey toward

freedom, you will learn how to dissolve the gunk/impediments in your spiritual motor oil. These are your blockages—things you want to get rid of in order to live freer. This gunk is radioactive kryptonite and will melt your engine, a.k.a. your soul, if not dealt with properly. That's why your uncomfortability is such a gift. Like warning lights on your dashboard, it lets you know something important needs your attention.

These spiritual engine knockings are such important messages. When everything in life is going smoothly, you may not give much thought to what's going on inside you. You may even forget to be grateful for every living day. Why bother, you think, everything is just fine. But then you hear "knock, knock, knock," and the uncomfortability blossoms.

Don't worry. You're getting a message that it's time to listen up! This gift is a wake-up call, letting you know it's time to clear out the gunk you didn't know was holding you back. Now you can begin asking questions like, "What are these impediments in my oil? Where did they come from? Why are they there? What are they doing there? What's their purpose?"

Good! Those are great questions. And now that you're listening to that voice inside of you, you're on the path to answers. Answers from Hashem. That's who's sending you the messages, and now you've got an ally, helping your car move faster, allowing you to focus on seeing the road instead of yelling at other cars on the road, the ones that seem to be in your way.

By now, though, you know those other cars aren't really the problem. Again, they're all messengers, helping you understand the urgency of releasing this stuff to a power much, much greater than yourself. You have an ally with you 24/7, 365 days a year. In good times and not so good times. Where is it? Inside of you. And this ally wants you to be free.

NEXT STEP

Next time you hit a bump in the road or hear your spiritual engine knocking, stop. Pay attention. Write down every question that comes to mind. When we're upset, we often find our minds racing, overloaded with questions—good questions that we might forget if we don't write them down. Once you have your list, explore the questions that came up. Look for possible answers in your toolkit, including asking for help from your higher power. (We'll get into this more later in this chapter.)

REMARKABLE RESULTS #2: Take responsibility for your life.

Newsflash! Like your physical ecosystem, your spiritual ecosystem works in much the same way to free you of unnecessary waste.

As you already know, the physical ecosystem is very straightforward. God created it that way. You eat; you digest; you need to eliminate. It's either number one or number two. The message is super clear. And just like when you were little and learned to be potty trained, well, the same goes for your spiritual life. It takes added awareness and training. Here's how that works.

In your physical ecosystem, when you've had a meal, your stomach feels full. So far so good. But sometime after the meal, you begin to sense a rumbling in your midsection that feels very uncomfortable. No matter how hard you try to suppress it and deny the feelings, you cannot avoid what needs to happen—a trip to the nearest facilities to relieve yourself. That's how your body's ecosystem works—it *compels* you to take action. And how do you do that? Basically you sit and relax and release, followed by a sense of serenity.

OK, the same goes for your spiritual ecosystem, also known as your emotional digestive system. Like that delicious meal you ingested, your day is going well; you're enjoying your journey. Then suddenly, you feel something uncomfortable. Maybe you get some upsetting news. You didn't get a job you wanted or didn't get invited to a party your friends are all going to. Perhaps an unexpected bill arrives in the mail and you feel financial anxiety. I don't have to tell you how long that list can be.

Your uncomfortability is a gift.

Hard as it may seem at that moment, you've just been given a wonderful opportunity. That uncomfortable experience is a gift. You've received a message. Instead of railing at the bill or your friends, none of which does anything for your spiritual growth except perpetuate more uncomfortable feelings, you need to simply sit. That's right. Just sit, like you did with your body when it needed to release something. Relax and listen in order to understand what is happening and for what particular reason. Hashem is talking to you and offering you release from uncomfortability. He installed this emotional digestive system inside to help bring you closer to him. This is part of the pre-installed operating system that we *all* came out of our moms with. It's time to start using it properly.

Aren't we always working to feel better, look better, smell better, improve our jump shot, our cooking skills—basically, looking to improve our life circumstances by all means possible? Except too often we forget about the most important means of all—at the foundation. It all starts from the inside, from the oil in your engine. Fix that and all else will follow.

Instead, most people go to war with their uncomfortability. They hire lawyers, do drugs, get depressed, get divorced, quit a job, fight with their colleague, stop talking to family members, on and on and on. Some commit crimes. Some even end their lives. When we focus our attention solely on the event/person we think caused our upset, we end up living in unhappiness, discontentment and chaos.

But you're waking up to the messages your uncomfortability is transmitting. You now recognize them as gifts. OK, they may be gift wrapped in doo-doo, but that's just the universe's way of getting your attention in order to help you get free.

What is all that gunk trying to tell you? "Release me, release me." And to get your attention, your spiritual engine starts to knock, making a racket. When you react with fear or worry, that's when the ego/*Yetzer Hara* aka Satan tentacles start forming around your spiritual neck, growing tighter and tighter. You can break that hold, but you need to release it first.

How?

"The stimulus for a lobster to be able to grow out of its shell is to feel uncomfortable... if lobsters were able to go to a doctor, they would be given a Valium or Percocet and never grow."
~ Rabbi Abraham Twerski^{AH'}

The solution starts with your willingness to take responsibility for your life, which also means taking responsibility for your freedom. Only you and God/Hashem can clean your system. He wants you to be free to serve, so give him that toxic, radioactive kryptonite (your lack) to handle. We mortal humans cannot do it alone.

NEXT STEP

Make a list of five things/events you worried yourself sick about—that in the end resolved themselves. Did your worry and angst help resolve them? Probably not. What did resolve them? Can you sense any guidance or help? Of course I don't want you to dwell on past troubles, but my hope is you will see a pattern that will help you relax when trouble stirs in the future. I want you to know on a deep level that you have an ally just waiting to help you.

REMARKABLE RESULTS #3: Let Go, Let God

Your spiritual ecosystem isn't as straightforward as your

biological one. Many more factors go into the who/why/what of blockages, but you can discover answers when you take a few deep breaths and relax. Your spiritual self is talking to you. Your soul is speaking the language of release.

So how do you do that?

"I got an unexpected bill." Relax your body; relax your shoulders. Set the bill aside for now.

Take a breath and relax even more. And surrender your fear and worries to Hashem. Try putting yours arms to the sky and say, "Hashem please take this feeling of financial fear away from me. It's bigger than I thought."

Breathe. Relax, relax, relax. Give up your worries to the universe.

In that relaxing, you start to recognize what's going on. What's *really* going on. It's not the bill, or the lost job or disappointing results. It's what you're *feeling*, and that's often some sort of lack. That lack can be all kinds of things. In the case of the bill, it's a financial lack. Maybe your partner ran up a credit card debt, and you want to blame her, but again, that's not the real issue. The real issue is the lack you're feeling.

Now's the time to sit and release. Relax, get clear on the issue and give it to the universe. Ask God or Hashem to take this off of you. Let go of all the anger, frustration, resentment— all those things that will never help you feel whole. They just mask what's going on.

Ask whatever higher power speaks to you and the answers will come. Relax, pay attention to the message and then release. You can't hold on to all that toxic stuff. It's poison.

NEXT STEP

Make a list of five things/events you worried yourself Start with something small. Maybe you have an annoying neighbor you've stopped speaking to. Or a coworker you can't stand. Sit with that and give it up to the universe. Let the tensions go in order to let something new come in. In the next section, we'll explore different ways of thinking and new options to explore.

REMARKABLE RESULTS #4: Live in a new way.

Let's look at a scenario from life with a couple of possible outcomes.

Scenario #1: Back to that bill, the unexpectedly high credit card bill. Automatically you have fear, worry, uncertainty. You start to experience chaos in your energy field. You react in the fog you've conjured. You become angry, and you can't see clearly. The fog becomes so thick that you begin to shut down. Your engine stalls, and that's when things get dicey. You react, drink, take drugs, get mad, blame. You cry and worry yourself into emotional exhaustion. Problem is, the bill is still there in the morning. All that worry and chaos, yet nothing has changed. You wake up to it all again the next day, and the next.

Scenario #2: You get that unexpectedly high credit card bill.

Automatically you have fear, worry, uncertainty, but now you have the self-awareness to hear the message, a.k.a. the gift wrapped in doo-doo. You recognize your feelings and thank the Creator for this gift of uncomfortability. And then you release it. You work on reducing the intensity of this issue by giving it to God or Hashem, and it goes from an intensity level of ten to a nine. With practice this doesn't take long, just a few seconds. OK, maybe a few minutes until you get better and better at this process. You get yourself down to a six before you go to bed and enjoy a full night's sleep. The next day you take a look at the bill and make a decision on how to handle the situation.

By taking spiritual action, I move on. I live life. I am free.

What happens then is you create some space between you and it, and when you do that, the solution arises. You'll be able to see the road in front of you, and boom, solutions start to appear. The sun breaks through and bye-bye fog! Ideas start to present themselves to you, like helpful billboards along your journey.

- Maybe I'll call the credit card folks and tell them I'm going to be a little late.
- Maybe I'll send them a hundred bucks.
- Maybe I'll return that item I just received but don't really need.
- Maybe I'll cancel a subscription for something that's not that important.
- Maybe I talk to a friend I can confide in, just to release the issue with a caring person.

The result is that by taking spiritual action, you move on. You live life. You watch clouds. You breathe. You love. You live. You live to love. You are free.

Jason was a client who was working quite diligently on getting freer. He came to me one day and said, "Jeff, I lost it last week. I was moving my business and the people doing my address change were not cooperative. And I just lost it."

"Congratulations!" I said.

He look confused at first, but then the light bulb went off. He knew I meant this was a gift, a message. But then he frowned. "Jeff, I want to be perfect."

To which I said, "Get over it. This journey is all about progress—not perfection. Recognize what you did that wasn't coming from your higher self—and understand that there's more work to be done."

Jason eventually got it. He's doing the work, practicing some present-full exercises. He's getting more into the moment because he really doesn't want to be that person who loses it with others.

Remember my story about my wife telling me I needed a thicker skin? And I said, no, I want to feel everything, out in the open? Yeah, that means maybe, from time to time, I'll lose it over something too, but that's OK. I want to feel it and get at it and release it so I can be freer. We always have stuff that goes on. Life will happen, right?

So what are you going to do about it? That's my question to you. You may start with complaining, then even freak out about it. But now it's out in the open, an invitation to change — to get freer. Go for it!

NEXT STEP

That famous quote by Albert Einstein I cited earlier? *"You cannot address a problem in your life with the same mind that got you there in the first place."* I'd like to upgrade that amazing quote to: "You cannot fix your life situation with the same level of **soul** that got you there in the first place." With an elevated soul, you elevate your viewpoint, which elevates your life.

Try this exercise, which should not take longer than 360 seconds, to start getting to a freer level.

I want you to go back to a very recent event that made you uncomfortable. Come on, you've gotten this far in the book. You can do this. It could have been as simple as someone cutting you off on the road or someone at work insulting you, intentionally or not. Could be deeper, like a recent disappointment. Please don't choose something too difficult. Like any exercise program, we need to start off with three-pound weights and build up.

Sit quietly and go back in your mind's eye to the moment, to the exact moment, right before you felt this disturbed and uncomfortable feeling. Try to see it as if you're watching a scene from a movie.

So, as you get to that moment of uncomfortability, picture the event, feel the uncomfortability and really, really feel into it. Now identify the feeling. If you need to use the Feeling Inventory, that's okay. Words, as you know, are important.

Once you feel a click inside of you with the right word (you'll know it when you feel it), I want you to thank the Creator for it. Say, *Thank you, God, for this feeling.* Remember the Creator wants you to be free.

Now you've got this message wrapped in poop that's grabbed your attention. Again, get clear and thank the Creator for this uncomfortable feeling.

Next, I want you to raise your hands in front of you up to the sky and ask the Creator to take this feeling away from you. Say, "God, please take this feeling away from me." Feel into it. Feel how inside of you is getting a bit lighter as you get freer. For now, I want the intensity of that feeling to just go down from a 10 to a 9. In time you can go lower.

You'll know if it worked if you feel a little better and less heavy around it. You'll feel less intense about it, 10% less. If you'd like to go further you can ask the Creator for a better way to handle or respond to this. Say, "God, help me to respond to this. How should I handle this response? How should I respond and deal with the situation?"

Now, listen. Listen for it. Got it? Good for you.

Remember this is about practice—not about perfection.

A TEAM'S CASE STUDY

I want to share a story about how working 10% freer led to small changes in a group that went on to create huge wins.

It started when I was working with a large company that was quite successful, but it was experiencing difficulty in one of its departments. Upon further investigation, I noticed the problem stemmed from too many people trying to drive the car. They weren't just driving, either. They were blaming each other for the way they were driving. Needless to say, the team was dysfunctional and not working together like an efficient pit crew. They were too busy criticizing each other to really get their jobs done.

So when we started to work on this, I first interviewed each team member. Not a pretty sight.

But then we began to talk about it, and I started to teach them that becoming 10% freer was first for them individually. They got that and began to understand their blockages. They were able to see why they were behaving reactively with one another. Over time, they got better at understanding themselves, and that created an appreciation of the other person next to them on the team. Ah, empathy awareness.

We kept at it, focusing on the direction of how we wanted to improve the unit. Eventually, there was a breakthrough in the team when one of the team members bought pizza for everyone and remembered to get a veggie pie for the vegan in the group. This was a small step, but it made a huge difference in the dynamics of the team.

They needed to come together or fall apart. Fortunately, they began to recognize that what they were doing and how it was working had not been for the greater good. When they began acknowledging their own blockages and understanding what they needed to do to free *themselves*, the team began to really work. In other words, through their own mini-transformations, they transformed the team. Today they are probably the single most successful team in the company. And what's really beautiful is some of them have become mentors to other departments about how working 10% freer can make huge changes for the company and themselves.

> "Good leaders create followers.
> Great leaders create leaders."
> ~ Rabbi Joseph Sacks[AH']

8% FREER TAKEAWAYS:

1. Pay attention when you feel uncomfortable. You're receiving important messages that can lead to greater freedom—if you do your work. Sit with them, relax and release them. Now you're just that much freer.

2. Take responsibility for your life. You're not a victim— you're a fabulous, loving human being with a lot to offer. It takes practice, but you can learn how to embrace the detours and bumps in the road and mine them for valuable information.

3. Release your problems, tensions, and worries to your higher power. You have an ally—24/7, 365 days a year. Embrace the messages these circumstances are giving you—and accept the help of your beloved ally.

9% FREER:
WHAT IS YOUR
PURPOSE?

By now you likely understand that the purpose of your life is *not* to get more money, a new spouse, bigger house, more notoriety and so on. It's not even to get more spiritual. No, the purpose of your life is to get rid of everything blocking you from your higher self, from living closer to God, Hashem, oneness.

This book is just a start—only 10% freer of those blockages. The other 90% is your ongoing journey on the road of life. Once you've started, momentum helps you continue to rid yourself of everything that doesn't serve your purpose. Only you can fix the roadblocks you encounter, but in the process, you'll start to enjoy clearer vision, deeper feelings, and stronger experiences.

Ready to plunge ahead? OK, let's head back to your car.

STEP INTO YOUR FREER LIFE #1: You're the fixer.

You're on your journey in your car, and you've gotten familiar with how it works and a bit more about how to repair what's not working right. You're with your car 24/7/365, so it makes sense that you're the one to take responsibility for your car. And besides, your car is not going to fix itself. (Yes, Tesla is working on that, but that's for physical cars.)

You're the fixer, the mechanic. No experts necessary. Just start with the gunk in your pipes and all that junk on the floorboards that's slowing you down. And don't forget to upgrade your windshield wipers so that you can see how beautiful the road is ahead. As you roll along, you have moments of magnificence, and it feels great being freer, doesn't it?

But there's still more work to be done. Every moment of every day is a door waiting to be opened to lead you to Freedom Town in the Land of Now.

The question really is how free do you want to be?

NEXT STEP

Pick one aspect of your life you want—or need—to change. Sit quietly and focus on that. What would it feel like to no longer experience that? Think of four alternative ways you could make this change in your life. Choose one and give it a try.

STEP INTO YOUR FREER LIFE #2: Find your purpose.

Life is a journey, and no one has "arrived." I'm still on the journey too. I know I'm not the freest person on the planet, but I can tell you I'm a lot freer than I used to be, and I'm on my way to even more freedom. I also recover from a pothole so much quicker than I used to—even if I'm surprised by it.

One of the reasons I'm freer is I know my purpose. It goes by the letters H.M.I.S. or How May I Serve the moment in front of me?

What's your purpose? To get clearer on that, sort through that messy trunk and get rid of the junk. As you decide what you need—and don't need—you will begin to feel more present-full and more comfortable in your own skin. And that will lead you closer to your purpose.

When you let go of the junk, also let go of trying to run the world. You know, that driving need to control everything in your life. That just makes it harder to live freer and prolongs your jail sentence. Let Go, Let God. It takes practice and hard work, but you'll begin to create experiences that lead to wisdom, the wisdom of *you*.

"Each person should see himself as though the entire world is on a delicate balance, and with one deed, he or she can tip the scales." ~ Moses Ben Maimon Maimonides (Rambam)

By the way, serving does not mean being Mother Teresa,

finding a cure for the next Coronavirus, or eradicating world hunger (although, that's all possible!). For me "How May I Serve" is as simple as saying, "Hi" with a smile and "Thank you" the next time I get a cup of coffee at Dunkin Donuts and recognize, in that moment, that all I need to do is stand in line. I didn't have to grow the beans, harvest them, process them, or any of the hundreds of steps it takes to deliver a delicious sip of hot joe into my mouth. I didn't need to open a store. I didn't need to milk a cow, have a farm, drive a truck. All I need to do is stand in line and say, "Half decaf, half regular, half skim, half this, a little cinnamon, a little vanilla," and boom! Presto! Coffee is handed to me in a cup by the servers who are also serving the moment in front of them, and that moment happens to be me!

It's that simple: Serve the moment in front of you. Are you raising it up? Or complaining that the person in front of you is taking 72 seconds longer than you would like to pay for her coffee? Folks, that is madness.

Your service can take any number of different routes. Maybe you're an accountant or run your own business. Maybe you choose to be of service to your family. As you gradually get clearer and freer, people will notice. And sometimes, one of them might say, "Hey, you're looking pretty clear and free. Would you talk to me?" That's when you might be of service to the next person to help them release or learn how to release some of the stuff that's blocking them from living a magnificent, wonderful, present-full life.

When we become freer one experience at a time, we allow more creativity to unfold. We increase our renewable energy to create our experience. It's about renewable energy—the renewable energy of *you*. (Yep, Tesla is working on that too!) And this source of renewable energy is there inside you waiting and wanting to be released. It's your oil well! Work on giving it the platform to be released and gush throughout your life.

NEXT STEP

We are all servers on the great highway of life. We are each serving each other. Stop and think about that for a few moments. How have you served today? How could you serve tomorrow?

STEP INTO YOUR FREER LIFE #3: Clean your emotional pipes.

You vacuum your home, clean your clothes, scour your bathroom. Well, why wouldn't you cleanse your spiritual pipes? It's nasty in there. Time to give them a scrub. You'll get a little dirty, but that's OK. The payoff is like barrels of oil, liquid spiritual gold.

Do you take aspirin if you have a headache, medicine if you're feeling clogged, or VapoRub if you've got a cold? Have you gone to the doctor? Had a colonoscopy or some such procedure? Maybe heart surgery or a stent installed?

Why would you do that? Well, you want your physical pipes and pathways to be clear, clean. Ever hear, "Drink a lot of water?" I assume you want to be healthy so that you can be free from sickness. Duh.

So take the same care with your spiritual pipes.

"Oh, why bother?" you might ask. "I'm not good enough. I'm not like Rambam, Tom Brady, Wayne Dyer, Eckhart Tolle, LeBron James, Paul McCartney, Abraham, Yitzhak or Yaakov."

What? You think they are the chosen ones? Let me tell you— *they* are not the chosen ones. *We all are.* The only thing Tom Brady, Abraham or Moses have or had was an understanding of their purpose, which led them to internal freedom.

Put another way, it's the hero's journey, and you're the hero. Along the way, you'll encounter challenges from opponents who want your energy and freedom. These greedy types need your energy to fill *their* broken pipes!

But take heart! Like we talked about earlier, those opponents are messengers, gifts. They are there to help you get free because without their messages, you would not know what to eliminate from your spiritual pipes so that you can be free. So as strange as this may sound, welcome their existence ... but only after you consciously decide they are no longer running the show. Once you're firmly in the driver's seat, accept their messages—and get freer!

STEP INTO YOUR FREER LIFE #4: Become a freedom fighter.

Would you like to love both the inside and outside of you?

Well, you can.

Let's do this next step together. Start by getting still. Close your eyes and take 3 slow conscious breaths. Then, say to yourself:

My purpose is to serve, and I'm here to change the world one blockage at a time.

I am like a plumber on a mission to clear out my leaky, corroded, blocked pipes. And I now live a freer life, releasing one blockage at a time. I am now on the lookout for micro soul stones that exist inside me or are starting to form. I want to work on eliminating them before they enlarge and cause inflammation.

I am here to be a freedom fighter for spiritual freedom for everyone. I will seek the understanding and training to pass my driver's test. The road I'm on now is so limited; I'm just going round and round. It's time to graduate and get on the open road of my life.

You can raise your vibration by releasing the blockages that block your music from flowing through you. Ever been in a bad mood and not into doing anything? Ding, ding, ding! Blockage alert! Ever listen to some beautiful music while you're driving in the car feeling fantastic? Ding, ding, ding! Freedom alert!

See how that works? You now have a way of understanding how to set your GPS to Freedom Town in the Land of Now. Which is exactly where you start living more fully.

Everything is there in front of you as a message from Hashem, who is knocking on your door to assist you and make your journey even more amazing. Traffic snarls, a long line at

Starbucks, a lost contract—they are all here on purpose to help you get free. Maybe you need to work on your patience—or your understanding. Maybe you need to release financial fear. You're the mechanic. Listen to your engine. Open the hood. Fix those faulty valves.

Are you listening and hearing the real messages, or are you still pointing to the pothole and blaming it for your problems? Time to grow up. Get out of the baby seat. You now have a learner's permit. Start driving! Gain a new perspective on life.

Let's not wait to be lying on our deathbed to finally open the door to truth and freedom. Forget regret! Regret sucks! Let's regret nothing. Let's be free. We're going to die anyway. Why wait for death to become free? More madness!

Get free internally and become 10% freer one blockage at a time. Along the way, all your issues cease to exist. You heard me right. Get free and *all* your issues cease to exist in the same way they used to.

NEXT STEP

What are you complaining about? Jot your answers down and then thank them for being gifts. This moment in front of you right now, as you're reading this book, took 13.8 billion years to present itself as a gift to you wrapped up sometimes in poop, other times with joy or beauty. And yet you're complaining. It's a gift, dummy. Everything is a gift, a ticket to freedom. Now think of ways you release these blockages and accept them as gifts.

9% FREER TAKEAWAYS:

1. Clean out your trunk with all those blockages holding you back. Some of them you can literally tell to get lost. Others take more time and attention. Get what you need to clean out your spiritual pipes—so that you can go on to find your purpose and greater freedom.

2. Take time to think about your purpose. Over the next days and weeks, pay attention to what resonates. Get rid of lingering ideas that you aren't one of the chosen and see how you can start serving the world today—from a simple smile to a deeper connection with your fellow travelers.

3. Accept Hashem's gifts. They may be wrapped in doo-doo, but they're still gifts. They are showing you the way to Freedom Town in the Land of Now. Start living there, even "as if" at first. Eventually, you'll wonder how you lived anywhere else.

Ask, "How May I Serve the moment in front of me?" (H.M.I.S.)

10% FREER:
READY FOR THE
JOURNEY OF A LIFETIME?

Y ou made it! You're now on your way to being 10% freer. You have the information and roadmap you need to start thriving throughout the rest of your life. Keep your eyes on the road ahead, take good care of your car, and you will find yourself continually on this beautiful journey. The world is always spinning 365 days a year, 24/7. The sun rises every day, and sets each evening.

Sometimes the weather is fine, other times rainy or snowy. Whatever, Hashem is there, running the world. Newsflash: You don't! But you can take control over your *reaction* to all the spinning and inclement weather. And with this understanding you'll find your road gets clearer, your car rides smoother, and life gets better along the way.

Every morning, we say the Amidah, all the prayers prior to the first one for man; we praise Hashem and the first line of the prayer for man is "You favor man with perception."

"אַתָּה חוֹנֵן לְאָדָם דַּעַת" My question in relation to this prayer to you is, **are you listening?** You have the gift of perception, a.k.a. your awareness level. Hashem gave you this gift. Use it!

As Rambam (also known as Maimonides) says in his book, *Guide for the Perplexed*, "Our goal in this world is to strive to understand Hashem to the best of our abilities." How we do this in our daily lives is to release whatever is blocking us from that. Addressing any uncomfortability we experience through our emotions is how we become free.

As we put this into practice now, we are using the 10, 10, 10 formula. We give away 10% of ourselves so that we become 10% lighter and freer, which in turn gives us the opportunity to experience being 10% closer to Hashem.

Our Rabbis remind us during Passover, the Exodus to freedom, that the purpose of Passover is to remember that Hashem released us. Today we are no longer in Egypt, but we still need to keep releasing ourselves from the bondage of self, the bondage of what is holding us back. Back then, we were slaves. Today, we need to ask ourselves if we are continuing to be slaves to anger, resentment, fear, worry. If so, we need to free ourselves. This is a message we are continually reminded of in our prayers, in our holidays, and every time we actually renew our love of Hashem.

We renew and replenish and refresh every Shabbat, during the holidays of Kippur, Sukkot and all the holidays. We make

Teshuvah (atonement). We ask for forgiveness, we renew, replenish and refresh. This is part of our DNA!

> ## "If you are willing to devote your life to continued growth, there are virtually no limits to the levels you can reach."
> ## ~Rabbi Aryeh Kaplan

Follow your path

This journey will never be a straight line. It can't be. You're learning as you go (like all of us), so your path will zig, then zag. It's only natural that along the way you'll experience a missed turn here and a detour there. But that's why we started with only 10%. Ten percent is attainable, which opens the door to even higher percentages of freedom. Once you've started on this path, the momentum toward more freedom continues on and on, if you allow it.

Not all blockages are biggies. Some are simple annoyances about the weather, traffic, that slowpoke in line in front of you. Others are larger—financial fears, health scares, love losses. Either way, we've got to keep working on them, day after day, one step at a time.

I have my own stuff I keep working on. One of the main reasons I wrote this book is to help me remember that mission, as well as to learn more about how to help others, how to be of service to my family, my community, and people anywhere on Earth. I want to be available when people come and say, "Hey, Jeff, I want to be free. Can you help me?" I want to practice more Let Go, Let God—and raise my vibration so that I can go higher and see more. I already know that when you see life from a higher perspective, you become freer to enjoy life and can better deal with stuff that happens.

As you practice living this way, you'll find times when you just roll with the punches. Like recently when a client dumped on me. I found I was not angry or resentful or vindictive. It was like that last scene in "The Matrix"—I was able to stop the bullets and respond with love and acceptance. I understood that my client was in pain. I was coming from a place of no expectations, total acceptance and unconditional love. That gave me the ability to not let my EGO (Edging God Out) take control, which gave my client the space to vent about a huge project he was working on. Afterwards, we came up with three liberating solutions to what was eating at him.

Time to bring in some interesting connections with letters and numbers in both the Hebrew and English alphabets. It is accepted in the Jewish faith that the number 26 represents GOD. Here's why.

There are four Hebrew letters that make up the word Hashem. They are Yod, Hey, Vav, and Hey respectively. Yod is the 10th letter of the Hebrew alphabet. Hey is the 5th. Vav is the 6th. When we add these numbers to spell Hashem, we get 10+5+6+5=26. In the English language, G is the 7th letter of the alphabet; O is the 15th letter in the alphabet; and D is the fourth. When we add these numbers we find that G-O-D totals 7+15+4 = 26. Now, let's get a little woo-woo. You ready?

EGO (Edging God Out) adds to 5+7+15=27 (E is the 5th letter; G the 7th; and O the 15th). The Ego always thinks it knows better than God.

Don't let your ego take place of the grace that is available within you. Why wait until you die to get free? Sure, we are all going to die one day, and based on what I've heard from people who've experienced near-death experiences, they do feel free. And they want us to know that so we *don't* wait for death to get free. Don't put off forgiving people and releasing blockages that have stood in the way of love. Get free *now*.

Don't get me wrong. I don't mean be a doormat. No, what I'm saying is don't be *your own* doormat. Don't step all over your path to freedom. Remove obstacles and let petty stuff go. And even if you do get angry and curse, even if you plot the revenge you're going to exact next time you see that person who "wronged" you, it's never too late. You say you want to give that person a piece of your mind? I say instead get rid of your mind. Purge the blockages to your soul. Get free to live a life beyond your wildest imagination—loving and free.

A new world experience

What kind of world do you want to live in? How about one with peace of mind? Wouldn't it just rock to have peace on Earth inside your mind, your soul, your magnificent you? That sort of freedom is in direct correlation to your spiritual condition, and your spiritual condition is reliant on your level of consciousness. The greater your consciousness, the greater your awareness and the freer you become.

This reminds me of a client I've been working with for a few years. Alex is married with children. The family takes vacations in the same spots most of us in the community do.

His immediate family is a very respected and prominent one with some big and bold personalities along with interesting dynamics and a fair amount of dysfunctionality.

A relative suggested we meet to discuss and possibly address some family difficulties he was having. During our first session I asked him how he deals with situations that are unpleasant and uncomfortable. I'll never forget his answer as his body tensed, tightened up as he said, "I white knuckle it."

Alex dove headfirst into the learning as well as taking action. Today he is one of the most free people I know. He no longer *white knuckle's* life's most uncomfortable situations that arise. He not only is firmly planted in the driver's seat of his vehicle, but he also masterfully navigates the potholes and bumps on the road that arise in his life with grace and ease.

It is progress, not perfection, that we're after. We need to be gentle with ourselves as we recognize what we recently said, did, or thought that was not of our higher self. Throughout our lives, we require spiritual maintenance, just as we do with our car, our teeth, our grooming, our eating, et cetera. We don't just eat once in a lifetime and finish. We do it again and again. And with your car—you take it in for service, fix the brakes, change the windshield wipers and refill your tank constantly; it won't do it itself.

Same thing with being human. We need to renew ourselves and take care of the maintenance of our life. And the act of being 10% freer and getting higher is in essence continuing to take the actions that you need to work on maintaining your physical, mental, spiritual, and emotional body that you're experiencing and living in this moment. Wake up and smell your life. It's the only one you've got!

Life is a joyous journey to be experienced. I'm sure you've heard it said when going through life's struggles that there is "a light at the end of the tunnel." In my experience, I know nothing about this light...not yet, at least.

Life's journey is the tunnel and sometimes, in that tunnel, life is pitch black. I remember that blackness all too well. I couldn't see the cars coming or going in any direction because my eyes were closed. Although it was a dark and scary, scary place to be, I asked for and received help. I continued to work on myself and helped others to work on themselves. I've recognized and seen first hand that this tunnel that we call life starts to illuminate naturally. Actually it was never dark in the first place. You see, Hashem's light is always shining. We just need to work on seeing and feeling it.

As you progress, the light within the tunnel begins to shine even brighter. Eventually, this tunnel becomes one of those beautiful English country dirt roads, where the trees are joined overhead and go on forever. The light shines through the branches and leaves. It's so magnificent sometimes that you can't believe it's real. But it is! Stop racing to the end of the tunnel. You have plenty of time for that.

In this sweet moment of the present, you have no issues. You can have a clearer and freer existence. You have the ability and tools to respond instead of react to life's uncomfortable situations. And within this freedom, you have the opportunity for genuine creation. Creation of what? Creation of a life beyond your wildest imagination. Freedom to love the life you're living. You now can live in the solution rather than dwell in the problems. You live in the solution because you are free and clear to do so.

So, what's your purpose of life? It has been said, *do unto others*. Fabulous! By serving the moment in front of you and making this moment better because you were in it and experienced it, you are fulfilling Hashem commandment.

For example, I see the Mezuzah's on our doorways as not some good luck charm. It serves as a reminder throughout the day that God is always with us and that we need to take action and remember our purpose. So as you walk into a room— we're constantly walking in and out of offices and rooms all day long—ask yourself H.M.I.S (How May I Serve)? As you walk out of that room and give the Mezuzah a kiss with your hand, ask yourself H.D.I.S. (How Did I Serve)?

In time, as you work on being 10% freer, it becomes like a spiritual E-ZPass that gets automatically refilled. Instead of being reactive when something comes up, in the moment you feel it, you release it. You get freer and experience Hashem to the best of your ability.

I wish you all to always be free and prosper. May Hashem bless you, your families and everyone you touch. Amen.

Letting Go of 10% Meditation

Congratulations!!! You've made it this far and you might be asking ... "Ok Jeff, I get and understand that the issue and solution are inside my mind. But HOW do I actually become 10% freer?" You might even be saying, "Heck I really want to be 100% freer!"

Hold on young Luke... You know not what you do not know...

As a first step to help you on your freedom journey I've included the link below to a free, simple, and short guided meditation. It would even be helpful if you're an advanced meditator.

JeffSitt.com/Resources

ACKNOWLEDGEMENTS

Words can never suffice to properly express *hakaras hatov* (gratitude) to Hashem for all the goodness He has bestowed and continues to bestow upon me.

Thanks to my ancestors dating back to Avraham, Yitzhok & Yaakov and all those who walked after them and before me especially Moshe (Moses) for his selfless pursuit of freedom for our people.

And a very special heartfelt thank you (תודה) to Rabbi David Asher (Author of Living Emunah) for his warmth and friendship.

Here also I must mention my mother, Gloria, and father, Eddie Sitt^{AH'}, for more than just teaching me, but for also showing me the meaning and importance of giving back.

An eternal thank-you to my relationship conciliary, Ester Jerome, for introducing me to Rochelle and who knew instinctively what a perfect match we would be.

I want to especially acknowledge Harry A. Adjmi, who saw in me almost a decade ago something I did not, that launched my professional journey. And to Amin H. Adjmi who believed in me.

Thank you to my coach, Linda Basso, for all her input, unwavering persistence and guidance. And for especially insisting I look into my Jewish heritage for the next chapter in my learning and growth journey. Also, thanks to Nazira Chabbott for her knowledge and assistance in helping me translate my Jewish interpretations, perspectives and concepts into understandable information.

No less important to embarking on this endeavour is the love of my family–my wife – Rochelle, Eddie & Millie, Abraham & Sara, Marc, Steven and the rest of my loving extended family.

I want to also acknowledge the many teachers and guides that have graced me with sharing their understanding and wisdom that has assisted me on my journey.

Lastly, I must give a special thank you for the many, many people, clients and friends who've shared their lives and struggles that have made this book both a mission and passion.

FEELINGS INVENTORY

The following is from the Center for Non-Violent Communication.

There are two parts to this list: feelings we may have when our needs are being met and feelings we may have when our needs are not being met.

Feelings when your needs are satisfied.

AFFECTIONATE
compassionate
friendly
loving
open hearted
sympathetic
tender
warm

ENGAGED
absorbed
alert
curious
engrossed
enchanted
entranced
fascinated
interested
intrigued
involved
spellbound
stimulated

EXCITED
amazed
animated
ardent
aroused
astonished
dazzled
eager
energetic
enthusiastic
giddy
invigorated
lively
passionate
surprised
vibrant

GRATEFUL
appreciative
moved
thankful
touched

EXHILARATED
blissful
ecstatic
elated
enthralled
exuberant
radiant
rapturous
thrilled

PEACEFUL
calm
clear headed
comfortable
centered
content
equanimous
fulfilled
mellow
quiet
relaxed
relieved

HOPEFUL
expectant
encouraged
optimistic

CONFIDENT
empowered
open
proud
safe
secure

INSPIRED
amazed
awed
wonder

JOYFUL
amused
delighted
glad
happy
jubilant
pleased
tickled

satisfied
serene
still
tranquil
trusting

REFRESHED
enlivened
rejuvenated
renewed
rested
restored
revived

Feelings when your needs are not satisfied.

AFRAID
apprehensive
dread
foreboding
frightened
mistrustful
panicked
petrified
scared
suspicious
terrified
wary
worried

EMBARRASSED
ashamed
chagrined
flustered
guilty
mortified
self-conscious

ANGRY
enraged
furious
incensed
indignant
irate
livid
outraged
resentful

AVERSION
animosity
appalled
contempt
disgusted
dislike
hate
horrified
hostile
repulsed

CONFUSED
ambivalent
baffled
bewildered
dazed
hesitant
lost
mystified
perplexed
puzzled
torn

ANNOYED
aggravated
dismayed
disgruntled
displeased
exasperated
frustrated
impatient
irritated
irked

DISQUIET

agitated
alarmed
discombobulated
disconcerted
disturbed
perturbed
rattled
restless
shocked
startled
surprised
troubled
turbulent
turmoil
uncomfortable
uneasy
unnerved
unsettled
upset

SAD

depressed
dejected
despair
despondent
disappointed
discouraged
disheartened
forlorn
gloomy
heavy hearted
hopeless
melancholy
unhappy
wretched

FATIGUE

beat
burnt out
depleted
exhausted
lethargic
listless
sleepy
tired
weary
worn out

PAIN

agony
anguished
bereaved
devastated
grief
heartbroken
hurt
lonely
miserable
regretful
remorseful

VULNERABLE

fragile
guarded
helpless
insecure
leery
reserved
sensitive
shaky

DISCONNECTED

alienated
aloof
apathetic
bored
cold
detached
distant
distracted
indifferent
numb
removed
uninterested
withdrawn

TENSE

anxious
cranky
distressed
distraught
edgy
fidgety
frazzled
irritable
jittery
nervous
overwhelmed
restless
stressed out

YEARNING

envious
jealous
longing
nostalgic
pining
wistful

TOP 10 BOOK RECOMMENDATIONS

- **Jewish Meditation** by Aryeh Kaplan
- **The Essential ZOHAR** by Rav P.S. Berg
- **Pirkei Avot** by Rabbi Yitzhak (ben Moshe) Magriso
- **The Untethered Soul** by Michael A. Singer
- **The Biology of Belief** by Bruce H. Lipton, Ph.D
- **You are the Placebo: Making Your Mind Matter** by Dr. Joe Dispenza
- **The Power of Now** by Eckhart Tolle
- **Wishes Fulfilled** by Wayne Dyer
- **As A Man Thinketh** by James Allen
- **Lessons in Leadership** by Rabbi Jonathan Sacks

TOP 5 SPIRITUAL MOVIE RECOMMENDATIONS

- The Shift (Wayne Dyer), 2009
- Finding Joe, 2011
- What the Bleep Do We Know, 2004
- E-Motion, 2014
- I Am, 2010

ABOUT THE AUTHOR

After burning through millions of dollars and taking his hands off the wheel of life, Jeff Sitt crashed to his lowest, personally and professionally. But it was amidst that wreckage of one life that a new one revealed itself.

This former CEO and 40-year veteran of entrepreneurship, who has built companies and achieved incredible financial success, has created a unique approach to leadership development.

Weaving together tack-sharp corporate insights enlightened by his commitment to faith and community, Jeff helps individuals and businesses arrive at their own sense of purpose, and in the process a renewed vitality, guiding them into small increases in freedom that deliver high degrees of success.

For more information about Jeff and his work, please visit:

Website: www.jeffsitt.com
LinkedIn: @jeffesitt
Facebook: @jeffesitt
Instagram: @jeffesitt

CPSIA information can be obtained
at www.ICGtesting.com
Printed in the USA
FSHW020052091221